Thomas Jefferson, Landscape Architect

Thomas Jefferson
Landscape Architect

FREDERICK DOVETON NICHOLS
and
RALPH E. GRISWOLD

University Press of Virginia

Charlottesville

This title in the Monticello Monograph Series
is published with the support of
the Thomas Jefferson Memorial Foundation.

THE UNIVERSITY PRESS OF VIRGINIA
Copyright © 1978 by the Rector and Visitors
of the University of Virginia

First published 1978
Second reprinting 1986

Frontispiece: statue of Thomas Jefferson,
University of Virginia Lawn, Karl Bitter,
sculptor (Frank J. Davis, photographer)

Library of Congress Cataloging in Publication Data

Nichols, Frederick Doveton.
Thomas Jefferson, landscape architect.

(Monticello monograph series)
Bibliography: p. 183.
Includes index.
1. Jefferson, Thomas, Pres. U.S.—1743–1826.
2. Landscape architecture—United States—History.
3. Architecture, American—History. I. Griswold,
Ralph E., joint author. II. Title.
E332.2.N53   720'.92'4   77–10601
ISBN 0-8139-0899-x

Printed in the United States of America

To our wives
Jane Root Nichols
and
Dorothy Griffith Griswold

Foreword

The history of landscape architecture is beset by difficulties arising from the protean character of its subjects. Architectural history is simple in comparison, for buildings of stone and brick are relatively enduring. Even when one falls into ruins, as in the Roman Forum, something of the original scale persists. Gardens and landscapes, being built of living materials, are ephemeral. They change from year to year as their elements grow or die. A designer's vision of perfection lasts but a moment, for trees and shrubs are almost always too small or too big. An owner imaginatively elaborates with the eye of hope, or overlooks excessive growth to recapture the memory of perfection.

When a tree has grown to such size that it darkens or endangers an adjacent building, or damages a design it was intended to enhance, a degree of resolution is required to turn it into firewood. Even slow-growing hedges eventually burst their bounds, narrowing paths and destroying vistas. When box has grown to noble dimensions, one needs a critical eye to see that it may have destroyed a harmonious relation to its surroundings, and an even more resolute heart to remove it.

The grounds of the Henry Francis du Pont Winterthur Museum in Delaware are singularly beautiful in any season. Wandering through them once on Halloween, I had the illusion that Mr. du Pont had planned them solely with an eye to autumn color; yet I knew from spring and summer visits that that was not the case. A perfectionist in every aspect of the decorative arts and of horticulture, Henry Francis du Pont (1880–1969) could never believe that after his death anyone else would pay as thoughtful attention to small details as he did, every moment of his waking hours. One day in the 1950s when I walked through the Winterthur grounds with him, I came to realize how aware he was of scale and size, for he was laying plans for moving various large trees that, while handsome at the moment, would half a century hence be jostled by their neighbors. We went equipped with a supply of stakes and colored tags. He would decide where a tree ought to be, drive the stake, affix the related tags to it and the tree, and move on. The next morning a crew of tree movers would arrive to carry out these instructions. His eye was incredibly sure, as the grounds of Winterthur today testify. His landscapes will survive longer than most because of his farsighted planning and his realization of the relative growth of different types of living materials.

The landscape that Thomas Jefferson created at Monticello was less fortunate, for when he died in financial straits in 1826, the property passed out of his family. Only in 1923 was Monticello acquired by the Thomas Jefferson Memorial Foundation, a nonprofit organization created to ensure its preservation. Under the direction of the architectural historian Fiske Kimball and Edwin Morris Betts, professor of biology at the University of Virginia, plans were then laid for the renovation of both house and grounds; but fifteen years passed before the Foundation, with the aid of the Garden Club of Virginia, was able to begin the restoration of the gardens. Ever since work has constantly been going on to bring the landscape of the property closer to its founder's conception.

Professor Merrill D. Peterson in *The Jefferson Image in the American Mind* observed:

Although Jefferson was the recognized architect of Monticello, the importance of that achievement, and of his architectural work generally, both from a professional and an artistic standpoint, went comparatively unnoticed until the second decade of this century. For a century or more, practicing architects in this country worked in a tradition of classical design, especially in public buildings, without realizing Jefferson's seminal role. . . . The corner was turned in 1913 with the publication of *Thomas Jefferson as an Architect and Designer of Landscape*, the collaboration of two professionals, William A. Lambeth and Warren H. Manning. The part by Manning on landscape was superficial. The major part by Lambeth, though far from comprehensive or definitive, anticipated the later canonization of Jefferson as "the father [Lambeth was satisfied with "godfather"] of American architecture."

The publication of Fiske Kimball's *Thomas Jefferson, Architect* in 1916 established Jefferson's twentieth-century reputation as an architect. This work was reprinted in 1968 by one of Kimball's successors on the board of the Thomas Jefferson Memorial Foundation,

Frederick Doveton Nichols, Cary D. Langhorne Professor of Architecture in the University of Virginia. Through numerous other publications, Professor Nichols has contributed notably to our knowledge of Mr. Jefferson's buildings. Since the appearance of Warren H. Manning's essay more than sixty years have passed, however, without serious consideration of Jefferson's contribution to landscape architecture. This is not surprising for reasons that I outlined earlier.

This book represents a happy collaboration between Professor Nichols and a senior landscape architect, Ralph Esty Griswold, who, in addition to four decades of practice in Pittsburgh, has been resident landscape architect at the American Academy in Rome and, for work in the Athenian Agora, at the American School of Classical Studies in Athens. Mr. Griswold has also been a research fellow at Dumbarton Oaks and most recently has been engaged in an investigation of eighteenth-century gardens at Williamsburg. The joint investigation of these two scholars has produced the first modern study of Thomas Jefferson as a landscape architect. It has given me pleasure to have an early opportunity to read and to introduce this welcome addition to Jeffersonian literature, which is appropriately published by the press based at the university he founded.

WALTER MUIR WHITEHILL
Honorary trustee, sometime
president, of the Thomas
Jefferson Memorial Foundation

North Andover, Massachusetts
April 4, 1976

Preface

Although the title *landscape architect* had not been created before Thomas Jefferson's death in 1826, he was, as will be shown, qualified for that appellation. Another title will be superfluous to Jefferson's *memoria in aeterna* but it will identify him with an art whose history began with man's effort to improve his natural environment. The development of that art was, through his reading, observations, and travels, familiar to Jefferson. But in his time the various artists who designed the landscape were known to him as architects, master gardeners, sometimes sculptors and painters, and more recently as *landscape gardeners*. This last title was assumed by a group of English philosophers and landscape designers whose work was more closely based on the natural landscape. As will be seen, Jefferson was greatly influenced by their literature and landscape gardens when he began planning his grounds at Monticello.

This was an entirely new type of gardening to colonial America, where Jefferson had seen only traditional geometric gardens at the plantation homes of his aristocratic Virginia friends. But, as in all types of design, Jefferson's taste, though founded on tradition, was innovative. Despite his preference for English landscape gardening he never fully accepted any predetermined style. His knowledge of surveying, architecture, climate, soil, and other elements of the natural environment including plants, useful and ornamental, gave him a background for design superior to any landscape gardener.

The purpose of this book is to show how Jefferson adapted his accumulated knowledge of landscape design to his particular environment, thereby laying the foundation for a distinctive fine art that was to become recognized in 1899 as the profession of *landscape architecture*.[1] That art has in recent years become internationally

[1] Frederick Law Olmsted, Sr., *Forty Years of Landscape Architecture*, ed. Frederick Law Olmsted, Jr., and Theodora Kimball (New York, 1928), p. 74: "The official use of the term 'Landscape Architect,' perhaps adopted by Mr. Vaux [Calvert Vaux, an English-trained architect] appears to have arisen between January 1862

recognized as a fine art, requiring in most American states registra-
tion for the right to practice. Jefferson could have qualified for the
right to practice in any state.

As a pioneer in that art, Jefferson's writings, drawings, and ac-
complished works are the source of all the ideas presented here. But
for the correlation and interpretation of this historical evidence, the
authors are especially indebted to James A. Bear, Francis L.
Berkeley, Jr., Eleanor Berman, Mrs. Edwin M. Betts, Julian P.
Boyd, Helen Duprey Bullock, Edwin A. Dumbauld, Fiske Kimball,
Dumas Malone, William B. O'Neal, Saul K. Padover, Merrill D.
Peterson, Millicent Sowerby, Mario di Valmarana, Walter Muir
Whitehill, and the staff of the Rare Book and Manuscript Depart-
ments of the University of Virginia Library.

---

and January 1863 during Mr. Olmsted's absence in Washington." Its first documen-
tary record, however, appears on a letter of resignation from the Board of Park
Commissioners of Central Park, May 12, 1863, which was signed "Yours faithfully,
Olmsted and Vaux, Landscape Architect."

Other firms soon adopted this title, but according to an article by Harold H.
Caparn in *The American Landscape Architect*, the official publication of The American Society of Landscape Architects (Boston, 1931), it was not made official until a
meeting "at which The American Society of Landscape Architects was organized
. . . at the Office of Parsons and Pentecost, St. James Building, New York on
January 4, 1899."

Contents

Illustrations

Thomas Jefferson, Landscape Architect

CHAPTER I

Early Days from Williamsburg to the Capitol at Richmond

When Thomas Jefferson first arrived in Williamsburg in 1760 to attend the College of William and Mary, he was a lanky, seventeen-year-old, red-haired, freckle-faced country boy from Albemarle County. His appearance was not prepossessing. This was to be his first long stay without family supervision away from his boyhood home at Shadwell among the beautiful Piedmont hills that were to play such an important part in his life. He was, however, already well tutored in the classics by the Reverend James Maury.[1]

In addition to his home-style academic schooling his instinctive love of nature made a classroom of his entire natural environment. In that classroom his only teacher was his insatiable intellectual curiosity about everything that affected his life or the lives of others. This was the source of his remarkable knowledge of natural phenomena.

It is also significant that in this remote environment he developed such a feeling for music that through his own determination he became much more than an ordinary country fiddler who, during his college days in Williamsburg, was invited to play at the Palace with a musical group including Governor Francis Fauquier.

Probably the most valuable early influence in preparation for his planning career was his father.[2] Peter Jefferson, an able surveyor and mapmaker, attracted the admiration of his son who watched him plotting his surveys at home (fig. 1). Jefferson's first-known ancestor, his great-grandfather Thomas Jefferson who resided near Flowerdieu Hundred in Henrico County, was also a surveyor, a position of high public trust and a distinction in seventeenth-century America. This first Thomas was probably the "Mr. Jefferson" mentioned as one of the delegates from Flowerdieu Hundred in 1619, when the first legislative body was called in the New World.[3]

[1] Thomas Jefferson, *Autobiography of Thomas Jefferson*, with introd. by Dumas Malone (New York, n.d.), p. 20.
[2] Ibid., p. 19.
[3] Marie Kimball, *Jefferson: The Road to Glory* (New York, 1943), p. 8.

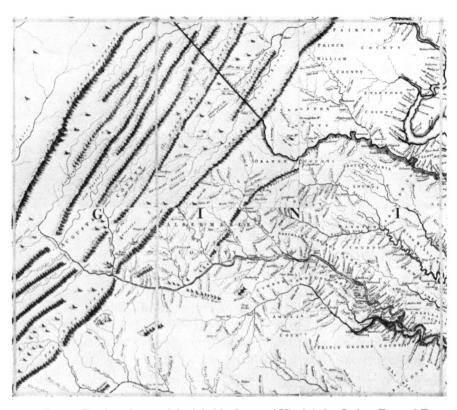

Fig. 1. Portion of map of the inhabited part of Virginia by Joshua Fry and Peter Jefferson, 1751 (Tracy W. McGregor Library, University of Virginia Library)

By the time his father died in 1757, young Tom already knew how to record on a map the shape of the land, the bodies of water, the forests, and the places where people lived in Virginia. For him, the knowledge of his native environment was not a subject for academic study; he was part of that environment with which he never lost contact. Jefferson not only inherited his father's surveying and drafting equipment, which he put to his own good use, but he shared his knowledge of the geography of Virginia. He became a proficient surveyor (fig. 2), a skill that he used at the city of Washington, Monticello, and the University of Virginia.

Having determined to study law in Williamsburg, this country

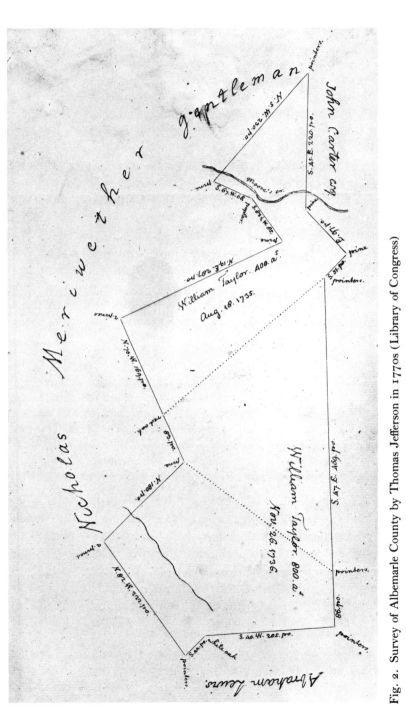

Fig. 2. Survey of Albemarle County by Thomas Jefferson in 1770s (Library of Congress)

boy had no lawyers in his family to recommend him. But the quality of his mind and spirit soon attracted Dr. William Small, who was to become one of his favorite professors.[4] Dr. Small, recognizing his exceptional talent, introduced him to George Wythe and Governor Fauquier, two of the most sophisticated men in the colonies. Soon he not only was playing music with them but was included as a social companion in their erudite circle. As a result, the boy's natural talents flourished.

Reputed by his friends to have studied fifteen hours a day, he was, however, by no means a greasy grind. He became one of a group of students who never missed a horse race, a fox hunt, or a hop at the Raleigh Tavern.[5] This group formed a burlesque secret society known as the "Flat Hats" at the College of William and Mary. His wit, love of music, and dancing were a part of his academic experience that helped him through his otherwise dreary undergraduate years in Williamsburg. At the same time he was already forming an opinion of the architecture of that colonial capital as expressed twenty-five years later in 1785 when his *Notes on the State of Virginia* were published. He said:

The only public buildings worthy mention are the Capitol, the Palace, the College, and the Hospital for Lunatics. . . . The Capitol is a light and airy structure, with a portico in front of two orders, the lower of which, being Doric, is tolerably just in its proportions and ornaments, save only that the intercolonnations are too large. The upper is Ionic, much too small for that on which it is mounted, its ornaments not proper to the order, nor proportioned within themselves. It is crowned with a pediment which is too high for its span. Yet, on the whole, it is the most pleasing piece of architecture we have.

Jefferson was here describing the second capitol, not the one which was reconstructed. Of the residence which he was later to occupy for part of his term as governor of the state, he said, "The Palace is not handsome without but it is spacious and commodious within, is prettily situated, and, with the grounds annexed to it, is capable of being made an elegant seat" (fig. 3). What he meant by "elegant seat"

---

[4] Jefferson, *Autobiography*, p. 20.
[5] Wendell D. Garrett and Joseph C. Farber, *Thomas Jefferson Redivivus* (Barre, Mass., 1971), pp. 20–22.

Fig. 3. The Governor's Palace in Williamsburg as reconstructed by Colonial Williamsburg (Colonial Williamsburg Foundation)

Fig. 4. Jefferson's sketch for remodeling the Governor's Palace in Williamsburg, ca., 1779 (Massachusetts Historical Society)

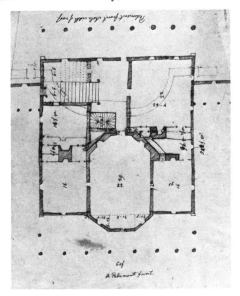

is shown by the sketches he made in 1779–81 for its remodeling (fig. 4). As for the other two major public buildings,

> The College and Hospital are rude, mis-shapen piles, which , but that they have roofs, would be taken for brick-kilns. There are no other public buildings but churches and courthouses in which no attempts are made at elegance. . . . The genius of architecture seems to have shed its maledictions over this land. . . . But the first principles of the art are unknown and there exists scarcely a model among us sufficiently chaste to give an idea of them. Architecture being one of the fine arts, and as such within the department of a professor of the college, according to the new arrangement, perhaps a spark may fall on some young subjects of natural taste, kindle up their genius, and produce a reformation in this elegant and useful art.[6]

Jefferson's determination to improve the architecture of these buildings and of American architecture generally was apparently formed in Jefferson's mind while he was still in college from the age of seventeen to twenty-one.

Curiously, he made no comment about the brilliant plan of the city, laid out by the gifted Sir Francis Nicholson with its unusual diagonal streets dividing the axial Duke of Gloucester Street to bypass the college at one end and probably the Capitol at the other (fig. 5). This departure from a characteristic rigid, geometric street pattern must have looked familiar to him when in 1791 he encountered the same sort of motif in Pierre L'Enfant's plan for the city of Washington.

The garden he frequented on his visits to the Governor's Palace as a student, if we can accept the garden indications on the "Bodleian Plate," was formally laid out in a diamond-shaped parterre (fig. 6).[7] This kind of garden, as Jefferson stated later in his notes on English gardens, did not appeal to him. Instinctively he abhorred straight lines in landscape design, preferring the undulating lines of his native Piedmont landscape. As a devotee of contour plowing, he realized the need to adjust farming to the curves of nature. With his constant admiration for the beautiful as well as the practical, it is not surprising that he loved natural forms. He disapproved of the formal gar-

---

[6] Thomas Jefferson, *Notes on the State of Virginia*, ed. William Peden (Chapel Hill, N.C., 1955), pp. 152–53.

[7] The Bodleian Plate, formerly C.30 in the Rawlinson collection of the Bodleian Library at Oxford University, was presented to John D. Rockefeller, Jr., and is now preserved in the Williamsburg museum.

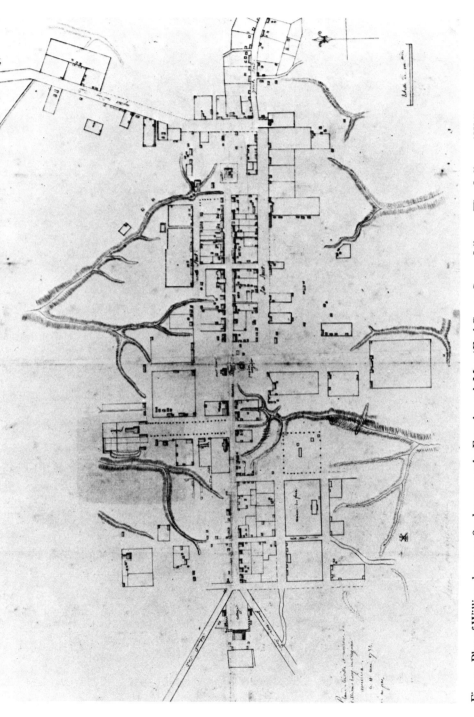

Fig. 5. Plan of Williamsburg, 1782, known as the Frenchman's Map (Earl Gregg Swem Library, The College of William and Mary in Virginia)

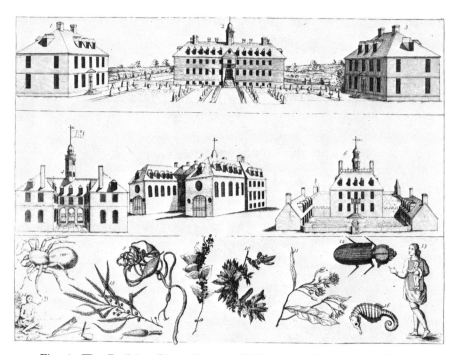

Fig. 6. The Bodleian Plate (Colonial Williamsburg Foundation). The garden indications are typical European engravers' imaginative decorations.

dens of the aristocracy along with the nobles who owned them. But he compromised this attitude when he admired free-form gardens which were fashionable when he was in Paris.

Immediately following his academic life in Williamsburg, Jefferson sought to expand his education by travel. With no other motive than to satisfy his curiosity about how people lived beyond his Virginia environment, he rode north to Annapolis, Philadelphia, and New York. In Annapolis this tyro architectural critic took time to record his impressions in a letter to his friend John Page: "The situation of the place is extremely beautiful, and very commodious. . . . The houses are in general better than those at Williamsburg, but the gardens are more indifferent."[8] By this comparison he reveals

[8] Edwin Morris Betts, ed., *Thomas Jefferson's Garden Book, 1766–1824, with Relevant Extracts from His Other Writings* (Philadelphia, 1944), p.3.

to us for the first time that he was aware of gardens as well as architecture. Although he made no comment he must also have noticed the diagonal streets connecting open spaces for public buildings in the city plan, also laid out by Francis Nicholson (fig. 7).

In Philadelphia he had himself inoculated against smallpox by Dr. John Morgan, who had recently returned from Europe with, of all things, an enthusiasm for the classical architect and scholar Palladio. Palladio's work was apparently not new to Jefferson but seeing Dr. Morgan's collection of the Italian's drawings stimulated him to a renewed enthusiasm which, even then in 1766, he related to the future house of his dreams, Monticello.[9]

Having received no academic instruction in any kind of design, he informed himself while a student at William and Mary by buying a book on architecture from an old cabinetmaker who lived near the college gate,[10] probably either Leoni's Palladio or James Gibbs's *Book of Architecture*. If this technical information was elemental, it developed his taste far in advance of his compatriots, who came to regard him as an architectural authority and sought his advice.

Without consciously trying, Jefferson was training himself by observation and reading for a broad conception of landscape design that was subsequently to be called landscape architecture. His youthful preview of Philadelphia and New York must have influenced his decision when he was given the opportunity not to choose either of these cities for the location of the nation's capital.

After college and his trip north, Jefferson returned to live at Shadwell. There on August 3, 1767, he noted in his Garden Book (fig. 8) for the first time the name of his future home only a short ride away: "inoculated common cherry buds into stocks of large kind at Monticello."[11] In this note he not only revealed his ability to budgraft but divulged this appropriate Italian name he had probably been considering ever since he chose a Piedmont site. It is a significant revelation of his great interest in landscape design that he started to plant at Monticello two years before he started building his house in 1769.

[9] John Dos Passos, "Builders for a Golden Age," *American Heritage* 10, no. 5 (1959): 65–77.

[10] Fiske Kimball, *Thomas Jefferson, Architect* (1916, rept., with introd. by Frederick D. Nichols, New York, 1968), p. vi.

[11] Betts, *Thomas Jefferson's Garden Book*, p. 6.

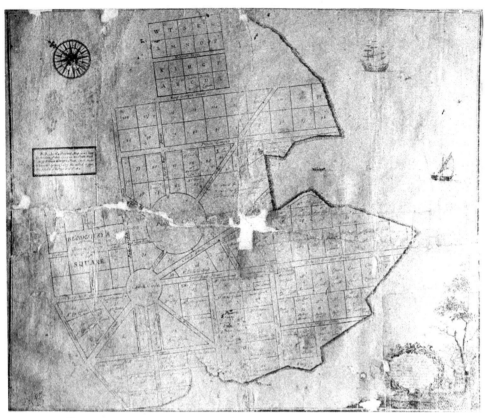

Fig. 7. Plan of Annapolis, Maryland, 1718 (Hall of Records of Maryland)

This house at first was to be strictly Palladian with two-story porticos. In Jefferson's earliest notebooks he generally derived details from James Gibb's *Rules for Drawing*, but shortly thereafter he refigured his proportions after Palladio's theories of codified proportions and law of architectural systems.

The house, one of Jefferson's architectural masterpieces, still stands on its little mountain, but the cherry trees at Monticello have long since perished, as is the nature of plants. His Garden Book, nevertheless, remains as an imperishable record of the diversity of the knowledge of this pioneer in the art of gardening, for him not a word implying the cultivation of a limited plot of ground in a traditional pattern. Although he was capable of thinking in the most precise and

Fig. 8. Jefferson's original Garden Book, 1766–1824 (Massachusetts Historical Society)

organized detail, this aspect of his ability was always subordinated to his comprehensive understanding of his entire environment.

The year 1767 was also the first year that Jefferson practiced law at the bar of the General Court of Virginia, to which he was introduced by George Wythe. During that year he tried sixty-eight cases that kept him away from home much of the time traveling over most of the western part of the state. Despite this absence he was not too preoccupied with his legal employment to neglect recording the events of his gardening: "Feb. 20. sowed a bed of forwardest and a bed of midling peas. 500. of these peas weighed 3 oz – 18 dwt. about 2,500. fill a pint. Mar. 9. both beds of peas up . . . Apr. 24. forwardest peas of Feb. 20. come to table." Alert to the aesthetic as well as the practical, he noted on "Mar. 23. Purple Hyacinth & Narcissus bloom" and on "Apr. 2. sowed Carnations, Indian Pink, Marygold, Globe amaranth, Auricula, Double balsam, Tricolor, Dutch violet, Sensitive plant, Cockscomb, a flower like Prince's feather, Lathyrus." Later, he noted when all of these bloomed. Not only annual and perennial flowers received his attention, but ornamental flowering shrubs as well: "Apr. 2. planted Lilac, Spanish broom, Umbrella, Laurel, Almonds, Muscle plumbs, Cayenne pepper."[12]

These excerpts are typical of his capacity for organized planning in the minutest detail (fig. 9). Never content with the act of planting, he was equally concerned with the dates of production when peas, asparagus, and strawberries "came to table" and when flowers bloomed. To him the process of plant production, like the construction of a building, was judged by the finished product. Nature was his contractor for garden building.

In 1769 Jefferson was elected to represent Albemarle County in the House of Burgesses in Williamsburg. In 1772 he married Martha Wayles Skelton and moved to Monticello. Rapidly becoming a leader in the movement toward revolution, he was also elected to the Continental Congress, meeting in Philadelphia. There, in 1776, he drafted the Declaration of Independence. Back in Williamsburg the same year, serving in the renamed House of Delegates, he drafted and presented a bill to remove the seat of government from Williamsburg to Richmond, the first indication of his interest in civic design. Although the bill was not passed, another bill with substantially the same wording was enacted in 1779, when the press of war made the inland location more attractive. In this year also Jefferson became governor of Virginia and returned as a resident to the Palace in Williamsburg where he had once enjoyed the hospitality of the royal governor Fauquier. From student-guest to governor in fifteen years is the measure of the speed with which this Albemarle prodigy rose to the highest office in the state.

His bill for implementing the move of the capital to Richmond is his first city-planning document. It contained precedent-shattering innovations reaching far beyond the traditional functions of a legislator or architect providing "that six whole squares of ground surrounded each of them by four streets . . . shall be appropriated to the use and purpose of public buildings" (fig. 10). He had observed this sort of planning at Williamsburg and Annapolis. In addition, for the first time in America, Jefferson separated the three branches of government in buildings on squares of their own.

[12] Ibid., pp. 4–5.

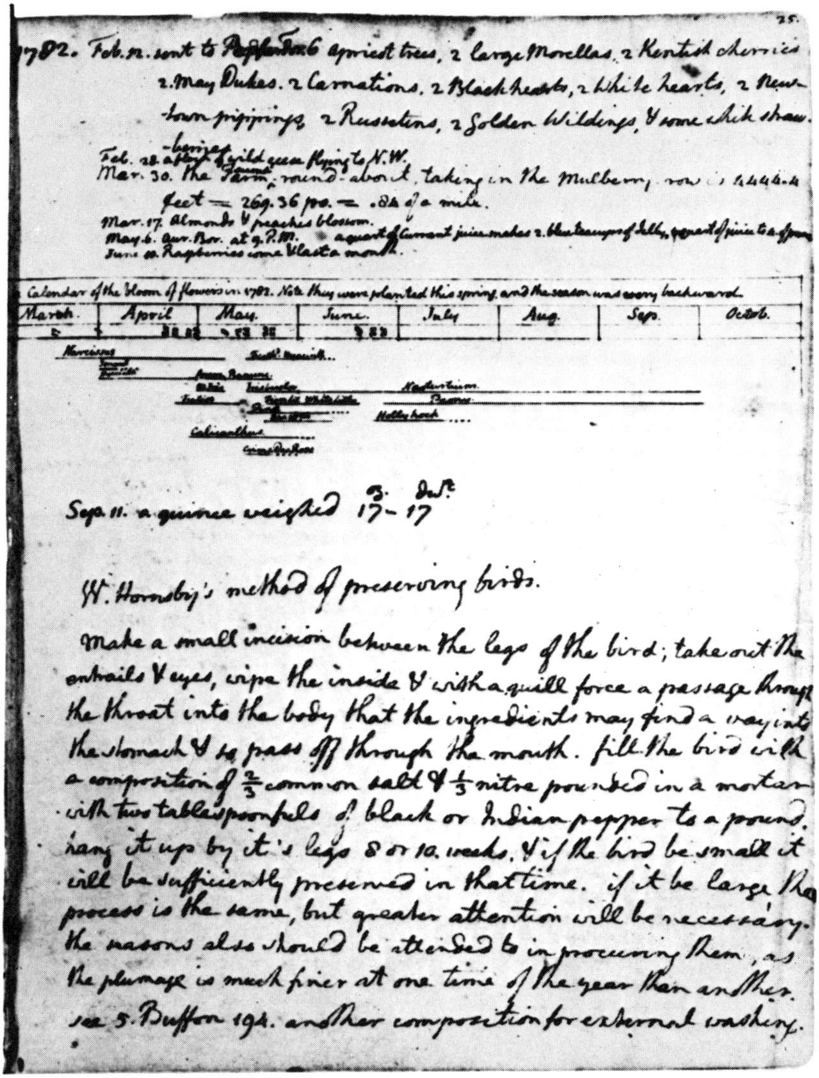

Fig. 9. Jefferson's Garden Book, p. 25, Feb. 12, 1782, chart showing succession of bloom (Massachusetts Historical Society)

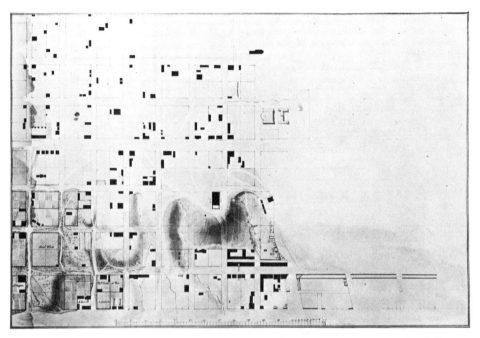

Fig. 10. Plan of Richmond showing the site of the Capitol, drawn by Jefferson, 1780 (Massachusetts Historical Soceity)

On one of s[ai]d squares shall be erected one house for the use of the General Assembly, to be called the Capitol, which sd Capitol shall contain *two* apartments for the use of the Senate & their clerk, two others for the use of the House of Delegates and their clerk, and others for the purposes of Conferences, Committees, and a Lobby, of such forms & dimensions as shall be adapted to their respective purposes. On one other of the sd squares shall be erected another building to be called the halls of Justice . . . and on the same square last mentioned shall be a public jail. . . . One other of the sd squares shall be reserved for the purpose of building thereon hereafter a house for the general executive boards and offices to be held in. Two others with intervening streets shall be reserved for the use of the governor of this commonwealth for the time being to be built on hereafter. And the remaining square shall be appropriated to the use of a public market. The said houses shall be build in a handsome manner with walls of brick, or stone and porticos where the same may be convenient or ornamental, and with pillars and pavements of stone.[13]

Admiring the Greek flare for dramatic site planning, Jefferson visualized the Virginia Capitol silhouetted like the Parthenon on the crest of Shockoe Hill commanding the entire city (fig. 11). Up to that time the city had been clustered east of Shockoe Creek on Church Hill and on low ground along the banks of the James River, the original source of the city's business. But in Jefferson's imaginative mind the Capitol was the home of the state's highest business, deserving a more commanding position (fig. 12). Likewise, in his estimation the architectural character should be more imposing than the typical Georgian brick domestic style which he disliked intensely.

The legislators quickly implemented their vote to move to Richmond, but the construction of the public buildings there was a lengthy process. First "for the selection of grounds, the choice of plans and building materials, five persons called the directors of the public buildings were appointed by the Assembly. At their first session in Richmond the Assembly named Thomas Jefferson, then governor, to the list of directors."[14] As Fiske Kimball points out, Jefferson's proposal for separate buildings to house the various branches of the government was without precedent either in this country or in Europe. Unfortunately, his personal influence was interrupted when he was sent to France in 1784 to represent the American government. In his absence the Virginia Assembly, finding his idea too advanced for their appreciation, changed it by voting to put all government functions under one roof as they had been in Williamsburg. This proved how far Jefferson was ahead of his time. But, for him, this was only a temporary setback. Ultimately, he saw his plan adopted in Washington, D.C.

Another immediate consolation was that the directors of the public buildings appointed by the General Assembly wrote to him in Paris asking him "to advise them as to a plan [for the Capitol] and add to it one for a prison." Naturally, he was delighted with this invitation. He saw the opportunity, even though only a single building was au-

[13] Fiske Kimball, "Thomas Jefferson and the First Monument of Classical Revival in America," *Journal of the American Institute of Architects* 3 (Nov. 1915): 473.

[14] Ibid., pp. 473–74.

Fig. 11. *Richmond, from the hill above the waterworks*, aquatint, in colors by Wm. J. Bennett, 1834, after George Cooke (I. N. Phelps Stokes Collection, The New York Library, Astor, Lenox and Tilden Foundations)

thorized, to design a handsome building. He wrote some years later, in retrospect, "thinking it a favorable opportunity of introducing into the State an example of Architecture in the classic style of antiquity, and the *Maison Quarree* of Nimes, an ancient Roman temple, being considered the most perfect model existing of what may be called cubic architecture, I applied to M. Clerissault . . . to have me a model of the building made in stucco only changing the order from Corinthian to Ionic" (figs. 13, 14).[15]

The plan for this majestic building was wholly his—the judicial and legislative branches all in one building that rose like an eagle taking flight from the hilltop. A nobler marriage of landscape and architecture had not been consummated in colonial America. It has

[15] Ibid., p. 474.

Fig. 12. Capitol Square in Richmond, ca. 1850, drawn by L. A. Ramm (Library of Congress)

Fig. 13. Maison Carrée, Nîmes, France (Rare Book Department, University of Virginia Library)

Fig. 14. Model for the Virginia Capitol, made in France for Jefferson (Virginia State Library)

been justly pronounced the most dignified and beautiful capitol in America.

That the inspiration for a porticoed building dates back to Jefferson's occupancy of the Governor's Palace in Williamsburg is suggested by five sketch-plans, sort of architectural notions he had for improving the Palace plan. Two of these sketches that he must have preferred were dimensioned, showing room sizes. They are all without dates, but Fiske Kimball dates them as "probably from 1779 until December 1781," when the Palace burned.[16]

In that case, the most significant one, showing eight-columned porticoes on both ends (see fig. 4), antedated a scale drawing he labeled "Virginia Capitol: Side-elevation—rejected study" (fig. 15). This "rejected study," made after he went to Paris in 1784, bears an unmistakable similarity to the sketch he made for the Palace several years earlier. The classical porticoed building he ultimately proposed for the Capitol in Richmond had obviously been on his mind for several years.

It would seem that this inveterate remodeler might have planned to remodel the Palace according to his sketch which shows eight-columned porticos at the front and back. He is supposed to have made this sketch about 1779. But then the state government moved to Richmond in 1780 and the Palace burned in 1781. Jefferson's dream of a classical building was transferred to Richmond where his design for the Capitol became the first example of classical revival monumental architecture in America.

The ruins of the Palace laid buried until in 1931–34 it was reconstructed by Colonial Williamsburg in its original early Georgian style with the help of Jefferson's dimensioned sketch plan which verified the archaeological excavations (fig. 16; see also fig. 3). Both it and the Capitol in Richmond, in different ways, are today memorials to an architect of unpredictable resources.

During his tour of duty as American minister to France, Jefferson's education received a powerful stimulation in the arts. As he wrote to Colonel David Humphreys on August 14, 1787: "I will observe to you that wonderful improvements are making in various lines. In architecture the wall of circumvallation round Paris and the palaces by which we are to be let in and out are nearly compleated, four

[16] Kimball, *Thomas Jefferson, Architect*, p. 138.

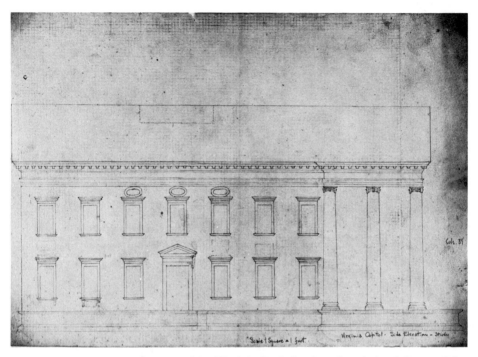

Fig. 15. Side elevation of the Virginia Capitol, rejected study by Jefferson (Massachusetts Historical Society)

hospitals are to be built instead of the old hotel-dieu, one of the old bridges has all its houses demolished and a second nearly so, a new bridge is begun at the Place Louis XV. The Palais royal is gutted, a considerable part in the center of the garden being dug out, and a subterranean circus begun wherein will be equestrian exhibitions, etc."[17] This experience, including visits to Italy, Holland, Germany, and England, was all he needed to make him the most knowledgeable designer of his time in America.

All through his formative years Jefferson had observed and meticulously recorded every aspect of his natural environment, including the aborigines, as he called the Indians. He had also watched the accomplishments and behavior of the settlers as they advanced westward into the territory most familiar to him. As a regional

[17] Jefferson Papers, Library of Congress.

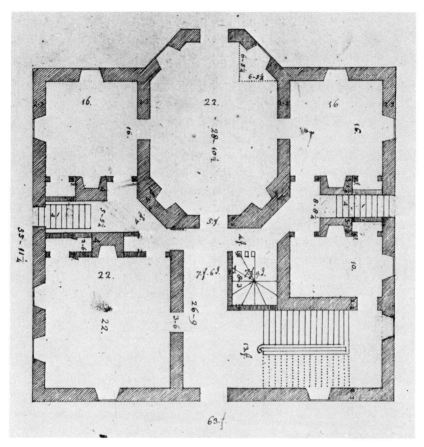

Fig. 16. Dimensioned plan of the Governor's Palace in Williamsburg by Jefferson (Massachusetts Historical Society)

planner for the amenities of mankind, his ability was founded on a comprehensive understanding of his environment. The information he had gathered and the conclusions which he drew from all these facts are in his *Notes on the State of Virginia*, published while he was in France.

CHAPTER II

Notes on the State of Virginia

Natural environment has influenced the living and building habits of people since the dawn of civilization. Its importance has varied only in degree, according to the intelligence of mankind. One of the measures of that intelligence has been the use of natural materials for building. Mud, a material common to all river-valley settlements, was as long ago as three millennia before Christ fashioned into bricks. Dried in the sun, they were used in the valley of the Euphrates for building homes and temples. Five millennia later when the first settlers began building on the banks of the James River, they used bricks fired in a kiln because they had learned that these were stronger and more durable. Thomas Jefferson was much interested in building houses of earth. His friend, General John Hartwell Cocke, actually built several such buildings at his plantation Bremo. They were constructed of pisé, that is, of mud puddled in wooden forms to form walls. More permanent and handsomer buildings were made possible by burned brick.

But for the James River settlers there was at first neither time nor knowledge enough to make bricks. They had to use wood, which was plentiful, as a temporary expedient. By the late eighteenth century, when there was no longer such an excuse for erecting wooden buildings, Jefferson did his best to discourage such perishable structures. In his *Notes on the State of Virginia*, he commented: "The private buildings are very rarely constructed of stone or brick; much the greatest portion being of scantling and boards, plaistered with lime. It is impossible to devise things more ugly, uncomfortable, and happily more perishable." Or not so happily—his own boyhood home, Shadwell, of wood-frame construction, had burned with all his books in 1770. Here is the nucleus of his prejudice against wooden houses, which he later tried to prevent being built in Washington. Instead, he pointed out, "the poorest people build huts of logs . . . stopping the interstices with mud. These are warmer in winter, and cooler in summer, than the more expensive constructions of scantling and plank."

He also noted that Virginians tended to ignore their environment in choosing their diet: "The wealthy are attentive to the raising of vegetables, but very little so to fruits. The poorer people attend to neither, living principally on milk and animal diet. This is the more inexcusable, as the climate requires indispensably a free use of vegetable food, for health as well as comfort, and is very friendly to the raising of fruits."[1]

These are only fragments of the breadth and depth of Jefferson's knowledge of natural conditions related to living and building as revealed in his *Notes*. It appears they were not originally written for publication but were compiled from miscellaneous data he had collected for his own information. Fortunately, when in 1780 the secretary of the French legation in Philadelphia asked a Virginia congressman for a reply to a questionnaire about the American states, the inquiry was referred to Jefferson. Possibly Jefferson looked upon this request as an opportunity to assemble and edit his accumulated notes, but he could hardly have anticipated the coincidence of being laid up by a fall from his horse at Poplar Forest in 1781, where he took advantage of his misfortune to answer the inquiries.[2] Putting aside the worries of his wife's declining health and an official inquiry with his conduct as governor and proving the validity of the old adage about the "ill wind," this indomitable man produced one of the most important books written in the Western Hemisphere in the eighteenth century, in part a composite of elements that affect the natural landscape. It was the only full-length book Jefferson ever published; it was, in the opinion of many historians, the best statement of his principles and, from the point of view of a landscape architect, one of the most comprehensive observations of natural conditions ever published. Some of his stated principles evoked considerable controversy but not those concerned with nature, which remained undisputed except by his own notes inserted from time to time in his personal copy of the authorized public edition printed in London in 1787 by John Stockdale.

Jefferson's efforts to keep the first edition, printed in Paris in May 1785, out of public circulation apparently stemmed from his realization that many of his conclusions about the state of Virginia might be

[1] Jefferson, *Notes on the State of Virginia*, p. 152.
[2] John Dos Passos, *The Head and Heart of Thomas Jefferson* (Garden City, N.Y., 1954), p. 24.

too stringent for the audience at home, and might reveal too many warts to its Old World readers. "Being Jefferson," concludes William Peden in his introduction to his 1955 edition of the *Notes*, "the author proceeds from compilation to speculation. . . . Thus he conceived of an 'empire of liberty'" in which he believed "men *can* improve their lot, if they will make the effort."[3] He made that effort. Much of what is attributed to his genius was, in truth, created by his own self-discipline, by the skill and training he acquired through hard, intelligent work.

The *Notes* show a profound knowledge of Virginia's geography, geology, natural history, aborigines, climate, zoology, botany, agriculture, ornithology, its people and their customs, laws, government, religion, and arts. This understanding of his entire natural environment, although he did not use the term *ecology*, was, nonetheless, based on that much exploited science.

Peden expresses this aspect of Jefferson's character succinctly: "From his mountain top at Monticello, overlooking the green and golden farmlands of Albemarle, he had peered into the vast laboratory of nature and had scrutinized like a lover the phenomena of the weather. He had been preoccupied with the mysteries of space and of the universe, and with that greatest of all mysteries, mankind. And for years, always the practical man rather than the dilettante, he had committed to writing any and all information which might conceivably be useful to him, 'in any station, public or private' particularly everything pertaining to Virginia."[4] *Useful* was Jefferson's most used word. Never a theorist detached from reality, Jefferson kept his feet firmly on the ground, a quality essential to any planner of landscapes.

Of his *Notes* Jefferson wrote in 1814: "The work itself indeed is nothing more than the measure of a shadow, never stationary, but lengthening as the sun advances, and to be taken anew from hour to hour. It must remain, therefore, for some other hand to sketch its appearance at another epoch, to furnish another element for calculating the course and motion of this member of our federal system."[5]

His *Notes* were answers to "XXIII queries," of which those perti-

[3] Jefferson's *Notes on the State of Virginia*, p. xxii.
[4] Ibid., p. xiii.
[5] Ibid., p. xxi.

nent to his qualifications as a landscape architect are discussed here. Query I, "An exact description of the limits and boundaries of the state of Virginia?"[6] Drawing on the information he had obtained from his father's surveys, he not only defined the longitude and latitude of every boundary but stated the source of their establishment, indicating his familiarity with the exact extent and legal status of the territory within which he operated. Query II, "A notice of its rivers, rivulets, and how far they are navigable?"[7] He revised the map drawn by Joshua Fry and his father in 1751, entitled "A Map of the Inhabited Part of Virginia" (see fig. 1), for reproduction in his *Notes* to accompany his own information as to the width, depth, and navigable length of the rivers. This knowledge became particularly useful to him later when he located the city of Washington on the Potomac River. Query III, "A notice of the best sea-ports of the state, and how big are the vessels they can receive?" To this query he wasted no time on useless repetition, answering, "Having no ports but our rivers and creeks, this Query has been answered under the preceding one."[8]

The extensive and irregular shores of the rivers and bays in the Tidewater area of Maryland and Virginia made possible direct communication by ship between plantation owners and London, thereby bypassing the king's colonial tax-collecting agencies and retarding the growth of cities in this area.[9] Defying repeated efforts by the English government to compel them to enact laws requiring the establishment of towns with the exclusive right to make shipments to London, the colonists successfully avoided these tax-collecting traps. They persisted in living separately on their own plantations with their own wharves for shipping their agricultural produce. This independence was the raison d'être for coming to America, and they were not going to have their efforts thwarted by English commercial interests. Jefferson shared this spirit of independence and always championed the man who wanted to live on his

[6] Ibid., p. 3.
[7] Ibid., p. 5.
[8] Ibid., p. 17.
[9] See John W. Reps, *Tidewater Towns: City Planning in Colonial Virginia and Maryland* (Williamsburg, Va., 1972), p. 64, where the beginning of town planning in America is explained.

own land in defiance of English coercion to build towns that were more easily taxed and defended. Basically an agriculturist, Jefferson resented all efforts to detach people from their self-sufficient homesteads.

Query IV, "A notice of its Mountains?" His reply referred not only to the Fry-Jefferson map for their geography but also compared their height to that of other mountains of the Western Hemisphere: "The mountains of the Blue ridge, and of these the Peaks of Otter, are thought to be of a greater height, measured from their base, than any others in our country [i.e., Virginia], and perhaps in North America. From data, which may be found a tolerable conjecture, we suppose the highest peak to be about 4000 feet perpendicular, which is not a fifth part of the height of the mountains in South America." He commented that this height of the Virginia mountains was "not one third of the height which would be necessary in our latitude to preserve ice in the open air unmelted through the year." The cited data were from the *Histoire Naturelle* by the comte de Buffon, the most influential work on natural history of its time. Jefferson owned several of the volumes of the duodecimo edition (Paris, 1752–1805).[10] Jefferson was always careful to relate his own studies to those of similar authority on the same subject.

For this scholar with a three-dimensional mind, the prevailing modern expression "in depth," used to denote thorough study, applied not only to the surface of the land but to its greatest known depths. Space, for him, was without limits. Query V, "Its Cascades and Caverns?" "The only remarkable Cascade" in Virginia, Jefferson answered, is "the Falling Spring in Augusta . . . a water of James river. . . . it falls over a rock 200 feet into the valley below. . . . Between the sheet and the rock, at the bottom, you may walk across dry. This Cataract will bear no comparison with that of Niagara, . . . the sheet being only 12 or 15 feet wide above, . . . but it is half as high again, the latter being only 156 feet, according to the mensuration made by order of M. Vaudreuil, Governor of Canada, and 130 according to more recent account." For caverns he offered as an outstanding example "Madison's Cave . . . on the North side of the

---

[10] Jefferson, *Notes on the State of Virginia*, pp. 18, 20, 262. Jefferson "years later ordered for the University of Virginia Library the 'Nouvelle' edition of 1799, consisting of 127 volumes" (ibid, p. 262).

Blue ridge" and illustrated his description with a scaled sketch proving that his observations of natural phenomena did not stop with the surface but penetrated to the depths of the earth (fig. 17).[11] Next, though he admitted that it did not fit into the present category, he described a phenomenon which he owned until his death, "the *Natural bridge*, the most sublime of Nature's works" (fig. 18).[12] He patented the land in 1774, refused to sell it for a shot tower, and in answer to another request to sell it in 1815, wrote William Caruthers: "I have no idea of selling the land [Natural Bridge]. I view it in some degree as a public trust, and would on no consideration permit the bridge to be injured, defaced or masked from public view."[13] Here he stated the principle of preservation of sublime natural scenery upon which the national parks were ultimately established. After describing its dimensions in such detail that a precise scale model could be made of the arch and its surroundings, he expressed his feelings with the fervor of an artist: "It is impossible for the emotions, arising from the sublime, to be felt beyond what they are here: so beautiful an arch, so elevated, so light and springing, as it were, up to heaven, the rapture of the Spectator is really indiscribable!"[14] It is fortunate that he is spared the disillusion of seeing how his "public trust" has been desecrated. It is easy to see that as a conservator of natural beauty for the enjoyment of his fellow man, he was a pioneer of extraordinary vision.

Query VI, "A notice of mines and other subterraneous riches; its trees, plants, fruits, &c." The amount of gold, other precious metals, and jewels, described expensively by early explorers as a lure for prospective settlers, was factually reported as of "no consequence." But lead was mined in southwest Virginia, smelted about a mile from the mines, and transported in the amount of twenty to twenty-five tons a year by way of the James River to Westham. Jefferson commented that the lead ore "is accompanied with a portion of silver, too small to be worth separation under any process hitherto attempted there." This is interesting because, later, a process was discovered

[11] Ibid., pp. 21, 23.

[12] Ibid., p. 24.

[13] Edwin Morris Betts, ed., *Thomas Jefferson's Farm Book* (Princeton, N.J., 1953), p. 335.

[14] Jefferson, *Notes on the State of Virginia*, p. 25.

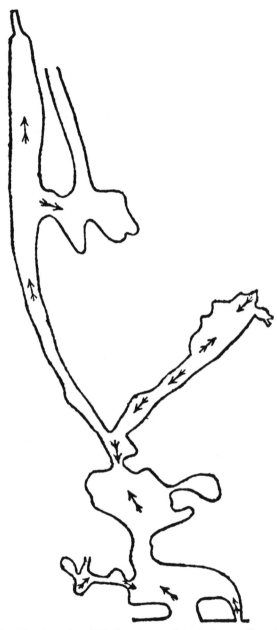

Fig. 17. "An Eye-draught of Madison's cave," by Jefferson (from Thomas Jeffer-son, *Notes on the State of Virginia*, ed. William Peden, Chapel Hill, University of North Carolina Press, 1955, p. 23)

Fig. 18. Frederic Edwin Church, *Natural Bridge, Virginia*, 1852 (The University of Virginia Art Museum, gift of Thomas Fortune Ryan, 1912)

that made it profitable to rip off old lead roofs to retrieve the silver content. Whether the lead miners took advantage of his suggestions for shortening the route of transportation of ore to the furnaces and of lead to its markets is not recorded, but his constructive advice was, nonetheless, freely offered. He also mentioned lead mines on the Spanish side of the Mississippi which, although they were not yet in United States territory, were not beyond Jefferson's anticipation of a Louisiana Purchase. Copper was dismissed as negligible. Iron mines and furnaces were reported in many parts of Virginia as was "mineral coal of a very excellent quality," but "the ccal at Pittsburgh is of very superior quality."[15] Knowledge of this sort had been instrumental in the earlier decisions of the English to drive the French out of Fort Duquesne in 1758 and to establish control of the Ohio River valley at Fort Pitt. Such information shows, not Jefferson's aesthetic interests, but his very practical regard for the environmental influence of nature's products. If, however, he could have foreseen the devastation that strip-mining was to have on the landscape, he would not have been content with expressions of disgust but would have found ways to control it.

Potential building materials—marble, stone of various kinds, slate, and schist—are described as to location, color, texture, and usefulness for different purposes. This information was invaluable to Jefferson as well as to others who were engaged in building. He was to make good use of it throughout his career.

Under the heading "Vegetables," he noted: "A complete catalogue of the trees, plants, fruits, &c. is probably not desired. I will sketch out those which would principally attract notice, as being 1. Medicinal, 2. Esculent, 3. Ornamental, or 4. Useful for fabrication; adding the Linnaean to the popular names, as the latter might not convey precise information to a foreigner. I shall confine myself too to native plants." There follows a long list including practically every tree, shrub, or vine, both deciduous and evergreen, that was useful for the purposes he had enumerated.[16] The ornamental plants listed were adequate for the art of gardening as practiced at that time, and the same list has been used by modern landscape architects for the restoration of eighteenth-century gardens.

[15] Ibid., pp. 26–29.
[16] Ibid., pp. 38–41.

As an example of the accuracy with which this list was prepared, his description of the "Paccan," or pecan, is typical (fig. 19).

Paccan, or Illinois nut. Not described by Linnaeas, Millar, or Clayton.[17] Were I to venture to describe this, speaking of the fruit from memory, and of the leaf from plants of two years growth, I should specify it as the Juglans alba [*Carya pecan*], foliolis lancealatis, acuminatis, serratis, tomentosis, fructu minore, ovato, compresso, vix insculpto, dulci, putamine, tenerrimo. It grows on the Illinois, Wabash, Ohio, and Missisipi. It is spoken of by Don Ulloa under the name of Pacanos, in his Noticias Americanas. Entret. 6.[18]

In addition to plants he provided lists of animals, both wild and domestic, with comparisons to similar species found in Europe.[19]

Then, in refutation of the comte de Buffon's "theory of the tendency of nature to belittle her productions on this side of the Atlantic" and the Abbé Raynal's disparagement of the whites transplanted from Europe, Jefferson defended the American Indians and whites strongly. Summing up his defense of the aborigines he said, "we shall probably find that they are formed in mind as well as in body, on the same module with the 'Homo sapiens Europaeus.'" Comparing America "with those countries, where genius is most cultivated, where are the most excellent models for art, and scaffolding for the attainment of science, as France and England for instance," he pointed out that "we produce a Washington, a Franklin, a Rittenhouse"; according to population size, "France then should have half a dozen in each of these lines, and Great-Britain half that number, equally eminent."[20]

For Jefferson this was no superficial patriotic boasting but the deep respect for the people and products of his native land which motivated every service he rendered to his country. When he planned, he planned for people with a full understanding of their

[17] Philip Miller (1691–1771), English gardener and botanist, was the author of numerous works including *The Gardener's and Florist's Dictionary* (London, 1731, 1765, 1768). Dr. John Clayton of Windsor, Gloucester County, Virginia, was an eminent botanist, member of some of the most learned societies of Europe, president of the Virginia Society for Promoting Useful Knowledge in 1773, author of *Flora Virginica*, and friend of Jefferson.

[18] Jefferson, *Notes on the State of Virginia*, p. 39.

[19] Ibid., pp. 50–52.

[20] Ibid., pp. 64, 62, 65.

Fig. 19. "Paccan" (pecan) tree distributed profusely by Jefferson (Frank J. Davis, photographer)

relationship to their natural environment. That environment, for him, included birds. "Between ninety and an hundred of our birds have been described by [Mark] Catesby," the eighteenth-century English naturalist who spent twelve years in Williamsburg studying and sketching the native flora and fauna. "His drawings," Jefferson thought, "are better as to form and attitude, than colouring, which is generally too high." Jefferson then tabulated the "Birds of Virginia" according to Linnaean and Catesby's designations with their popular names as well.[21] The man who ultimately was to design the University of Virginia was sensitive to every aspect of the flora and fauna of the natural environment he chose for its location.

Query VII, "A notice of all what can increase the progress of human knowledge?"Under this heading Jefferson included "climate," the environmental element with which he, as an agriculturist, was most vitally concerned. "I have taken five years' observations, to wit, from 1772 to 1777, made in Williamsburg and its neighbourhood, have reduced them to an average for every month in the year, and stated those averages in the following table, adding an analytical view of the winds during the same period."[22] Of this accomplishment, Edward T. Martin, in his *Thomas Jefferson, Scientist*, says, "With the possible exception of agriculture, gardening, and allied matters, no other scientific field held Jefferson's interest like meteorology, in which he appears to have made himself the best-informed American of his day. Even before the Revolutionary War he held that knowledge of the weather is to be accurately established only through simultaneous observations made at considerable distances apart. In this he was far in advance of the practices of his time."[23]

The various instruments for calculating weather that Jefferson built into Monticello are most interesting (figs. 20, 21). Again, not content with science in the abstract, he noted the effect of the weather on plant life: "if we may believe travellers, it becomes warmer there [the slopes from the Allegheny Mountains to the Mississippi] than it is in the same latitude on the sea side. Their testimony is strengthened by the vegetables and animals which subsist and multiply there naturally, and do not on our sea coast. Thus Catalpas grow spontaneously on the Missisipi."[24] In all his planning, weather controlled his design; hence the covered passages at the University of Virginia, "to give dry communication between all the schools."[25]

[21] Ibid., pp. 65, 66–70.
[22] Ibid., p. 73.
[23] Ibid., p. 278.
[24] Ibid., p. 75.
[25] Andrew A. Lipscomb and Albert A. Bergh, *Writings of Thomas Jefferson* (Monticello edition: Washington, D.C. 1903), 12: 387–88.

Fig. 20. Wind compass designed by Jefferson and installed at Monticello (Thomas Jefferson Memorial Foundation, Edwin S. Roseberry, photographer)

Fig. 21. Weather vane designed by Jefferson and set up at Monticello (Thomas Jefferson Memorial Foundation, Edwin S. Rosenberry, photographer)

The specific tables of his observations must have been as useful to the other farmers and gardeners of Virginia as they were to him at Monticello. Probably no landscape architect has ever planned any project with a greater knowledge of the effects of weather on his design than Jefferson showed at Monticello and the University of Virginia.

Query XI, "A description of the Indians established in that state?"[26] Jefferson must have been most happy to respond to this question because he admired the aborigines and studied their ways of living with the greatest respect. He produced tables showing their locations, tribes, chief towns, and warriors under the dates of 1607–69. He brought these up to date with information for 1759, 1764, 1768, and 1779, saying, "I will now proceed to state the nations and numbers of the Aborigines which still exist in a respectable and independant form."[27]

Query XII, "A notice of the counties, cities, townships, and villages?"[28] Answers to this query merely widened the scope of his familiarity with the political geography of his home state.

Query XIII, "The constitution of the state, and its several charters?" How he must have enjoyed this opportunity to express his philosophy of democratic government compared to a monarchy! He was under no illusions about the power of government of any kind to regulate men's motives. "In Great-Britain it is said their constitution relies on the house of commons for honesty, and the lords for wisdom; which would by a rational reliance if honesty were to be bought with money, and if wisdom were hereditary. . . . Human nature is the same on every side of the Atlantic, and will be alike influenced by the same causes."[29] For students of landscape architecture who are destined to work with government agencies there is much wisdom in these observations. Jefferson put his own theories to the test of practical experience before he sought to influence others to his point of view.

Query XIV, "The administration of justice and description of the laws?"[30] As a profound student of law, Jefferson was in his own

[26] Jefferson, *Notes on the State of Virginia*, p. 92.
[27] Ibid., p. 102.
[28] Ibid., p. 108.
[29] Ibid., pp. 110, 119–21.
[30] Ibid., p. 130.

professional field in his answers to this, as well as to many similar questions with which he was confronted in the later planning of the capital of Washington. Would that today's educators and legislators were as wise as Jefferson when he wrote:

The learning of Greek and Latin, I am told, is going into disuse in Europe. I know not what their manner and occupations may call for; but it would be very ill-judged in us to follow their example in this instance. There is a certain period of life, say from eight to fifteen or sixteen years of age, when the mind, like the body, is not yet firm enough for laborious and close operations. If applied to such, it falls an early victim to premature exertion; exhibiting indeed at first, in these young and tender subjects, the flattering appearance of their being men while they are yet children, but ending in reducing them to be children when they should be men. . . . History by apprising them of the past will enable them to judge of the future; . . . it will qualify them as judges of the actions and designs of men; it will enable them to know ambition under every disguise it may assume; and knowing it, to defeat its views.[31]

Using this query as an opening for citing his vision for the broadening of the state constitution to include the arts, he wrote, "Lastly, it is proposed, by a bill in this revisal, to begin a public library and gallery, by laying out a certain sum annually in books, painting, and statues."[32] His conception of these objects as an essential part of democratic education was far in advance of American political thinking.

Query XV, "The Colleges and Public Establishments, the Roads, Buildings &c.?" Explaining that "the college of William and Mary is the only public seminary of learning in this state," he suggested that the institution was not fulfilling its proper purpose, because of the lack of revenue and because "the admission of the learners of Latin and Greek filled the College with children."[33] He said nothing about roads because, compared with Europe, there were none, although there were waterways. On the subject of domestic architecture, which has become a primary problem of the federal government, he had much to say, as we have seen.

Undoubtedly, Jefferson's prejudice against wooden structures

[31] Ibid., pp. 147–48.
[32] Ibid., p. 149.
[33] Ibid., p. 150.

grew out of his reverence for classical buildings of masonry construction. He visualized America as a modern Rome, but he was to come to a rude awakening when he faced the realities of building the national capital. Yet in every compromise he had to make for expediency he held steadfastly to his idea when he designed for himself or institutions over which he had control. Were he to return today he would be gratified to find his own structures still standing as testimony to the correctness of his thinking. But he would also be surprised to see how many buildings of "scantling and plank" have persisted beyond his prediction of a fifty-year endurance.

CHAPTER III

The City of Washington

The capital of Washington is a monument to Jefferson's magnificent vision. He was indirectly responsible for its location on the Potomac River and for its basic site planning there. He also established its architectural and landscape character. Although many skills were employed in its development, his guiding influence and persistent management united them all. During twenty-six years of his life, from the age of forty to sixty-six, his energies were often devoted in one way or another to promoting and perfecting a new capital for a new type of government created for a new nation. No exact precedent for such a city existed elsewhere in the world. Its development was concomitant with the career of its tenacious supervisor; Jefferson was the man who followed through, as a member of the Continental Congress, 1783–84; secretary of state under President Washington, 1789–94; vice-president for President John Adams, 1797–1801; and president of the United States, 1801–9.

It must be realized that professional city planning as practiced today had not yet emerged from the long-established art of architecture and science of military engineering which had for centuries been responsible for the design of all the famous European cities. Jefferson had seen many of these cities and made notes on their design. He had also seen how Francis Nicholson, once governor of Maryland and Virginia, had used this precedent for the planning of Annapolis and Williamsburg. But, like their European predecessors, these towns were created under a monarchy, as were the new nation's most centrally located cities, Philadelphia and New York.

The city of Washington was the first attempt to plan a national capital for a democratic form of government on a site deliberately selected for that purpose. The planning for three branches of government—executive, legislative, and judicial—was a totally new experience in city planning. Except for the villages of Carrollsburg and Georgetown that bracketed the proposed area for the city, there were no habitations; it was a primitive piece of undeveloped ground.

The most convincing documentary evidence of Jefferson's contribution to the development of Washington is the compilation of his papers on this subject by Saul K. Padover. This book was published by the United States Department of the Interior in 1946 with a preface by Secretary Harold C. Ickes, who lauded "Thomas Jefferson, the many-sided genius who, among other things also helped to plan the Capital City of the Nation" and recommended the book "to those who are interested not merely in Jefferson but also in city planning and in the early history of our country."[1]

Supplementing this tribute, Charles W. Porter said in his introduction: "A product of this work has been a collection of notes and Jefferson correspondence which portrays the versatile Jefferson as one of our earlier and most successful city planners. . . . The best example of the Renaissance type of man produced in this country, Jefferson with his encyclopedic mind comprehended all interests, from bridges, roads, and the planting of trees to the manner of securing the bars in the city jail."[2]

The reference to Jefferson as a "Renaissance type of man" places him in a category of artists whose skill included every aspect of design affecting human environment. Calling him a city planner was using a modern professional specialization unknown to him but intended to broaden the record of his accomplishments. Repugnant as the evils of city life were to him, he must have made a great concession in his antiurban philosophy to devote so much time to creating the national capital. Having made the compromise, however, he determined to make it as beautiful and serviceable as possible, a most fortunate decision for the development of the arts in this country.

Watching carefully the votes of Congress for their preference of location between the Hudson, Delaware, or Potomac rivers, Jefferson wrote the governor of Virginia in 1783: "The first obtained scarcely any voices; the Delaware obtained seven [of thirteen]. This of course put Potomac out of the way." But when dissension arose about what point on the Delaware was intended, Jefferson sensed that this meant "unhinging the first determination and leaving the whole matter open for discussion at some future day." Before that day

[1] Saul K. Padover, *Thomas Jefferson and the National Capital . . . , 1783–1818* (Washington, D.C., 1946), Preface.

[2] Ibid., pp. xxxiii, xxxv.

arrived, Jefferson moved with the utmost speed to alter "what had at first appeared to be decided against us." Though he wrote to James Madison in 1784, "I fear that our chance is at this time desperate," he did not give up. He immediately drafted a resolution for the legislatures of Maryland and Virginia proposing that the two states concur in offering to erect "buildings for the immediate accomodation of the Congress of the United States on the lands on Potowmac offered to be ceded to them by these two states, & particularly on such parts of them as they shall have reason to believe will be most agreeable to the Congress."[3]

By this timely action Jefferson crystallized the idea of building on the Potomac, an action that was debated for the next six years while he was in France. Finally after his return he was able to write to James Monroe in 1790: "The bill for removing the federal government to Philadelphia for 10. years & then to Georgetown has at length passed both houses. The offices are to be removed [from New York] before the first of December."[4]

That Jefferson already had his own ideas for the precise location of the federal city on the Potomac in relation to Georgetown is graphically recorded by a plan from his own hand in 1791 (fig. 22). A letter he wrote to President Washington in 1790 probably represents the practical advantages recited in support of his choice; these were based primarily on the natural conditions of the Potomac and Anacostia rivers at almost the point where the city ultimately developed.[5] Definitely prejudiced in favor of a location in his home state, Jefferson, nevertheless, exercised the broadest kind of national planning, one far in advance of any professional designation used up to that time.

To Charles Carroll, a major landowner at the proposed site and potential commissioner, he wrote a memorandum, forwarding it through the hands of the president, initiating the terms of conveyance for the "lands as the President shall designate for the site of the public buildings, public walks, streets, &c., to remain for the use of the United States. . . . the President (without any further legislation from Congress) may proceed to lay out the town immediately

[3] Ibid., pp. 1–2, 4, 5–6.
[4] Ibid., p. 19.
[5] Ibid., p. 28.

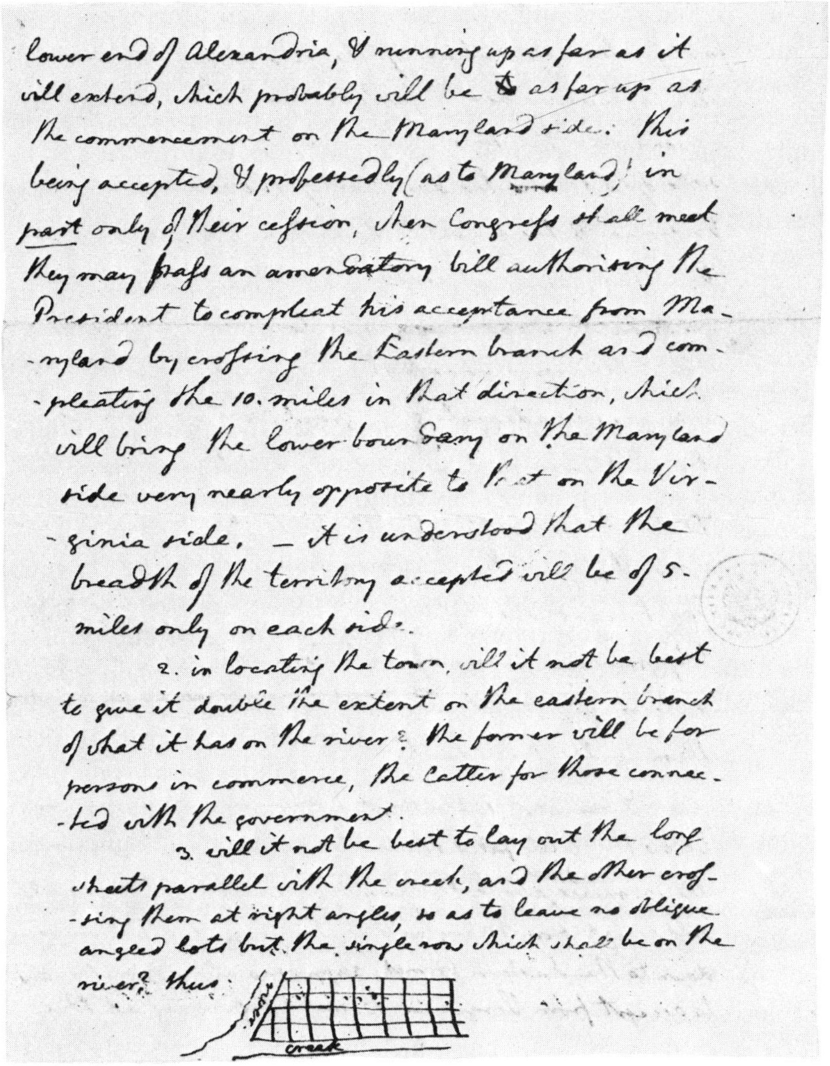

lower end of Alexandria, & running up as far as it
will extend, which probably will be ☒ as far up as
the commencement on the Maryland side. This
being accepted, & professedly (as to Maryland) in
part only of their cession, when Congress shall meet
they may pass an amendatory bill authorising the
President to compleat his acceptance from Ma-
-ryland by crossing the Eastern branch and com-
-pleating the 10. miles in that direction, which
will bring the lower boundary on the Maryland
side very nearly opposite to ⟨that⟩ on the Vir-
-ginia side, — It is understood that the
breadth of the territory accepted will be of 5.
miles only on each side.
  2. in locating the town, will it not be best
to give it double the extent on the eastern branch
of what it has on the river? the former will be for
persons in commerce, the latter for those connec-
-ted with the government.
  3. will it not be best to lay out the long
sheets parallel with the creek, and the other cros-
-sing them at right angles, so as to leave no oblique
angled lots but the single row which shall be on the
river? thus:

creek

Fig. 22. Sketch plan for the national capital on the site of Carrollsburg by Jefferson
(Library of Congress)

into 1, public lots; 2 public walks and gardens; 3 private lots for sale; 4 streets." In this outline of the president's initial authority, Jefferson, as secretary of state, also laid out the program for the planning of the future city. That program specified "a territory not exceeding 10. miles square (or, I presume, 100 square miles in any form) to be located by metes and bounds." For this ten-miles-square federal district, some of the original boundary stones still stand as installed in 1791.[6]

According to "the Residence act" the president was to appoint the commissioners and instruct them that they were to purchase or accept "'such quantity of land on the E. side of the river as [he] shall deem *proper for the U.S.*' viz. for the federal Capitol, the offices, the President's house & gardens, the town house, Market house, publick walks, hospital." For each of these units Jefferson designated the number of squares required "for the town: and I have no doubt it is the wish, & perhaps expectation. in that case it will be laid out in lots & streets. I should propose these to be at right angles as in Philadelphia, & that no street be narrower than 100. feet, with foot-ways of 15. feet where a street is long & level." Obviously, his conception of the future city at this time was based on the conventional gridiron plan with which he was familiar. For Jeffersonville, Indiana, he provided Governor William Henry Harrison with a gridiron plan which kept every other square open for parks or public buildings. When the town was built in 1802 the checkerboard pattern was followed, but most of the open squares were sold off and built up. In 1804 he recommended a similar plan to Governor William C. C. Claiborne for the capital of Mississippi, and in 1821 Jackson was so laid out.[7] In 1790, as the only planner of any sort in the national picture, he was doing his best to get the city under way before Congress had a chance to change its mind on the location.

"The Commissioners," he said, "should have some taste in architecture, because they may have to decide between different plans." He was anticipating the necessity of a competition for the design of the Capitol. His opinions for building restrictions, which he ad-

[6] Ibid., pp. 29–30.
[7] Ibid., pp. 30–31; *Indiana Works Progress Guide* (New York, 1941), p. 393; *Mississippi Writers Guide* (New York, 1938), p. 211.

mitted were "an object for Legislation," anticipated many that were adopted later:

I doubt much whether the obligation to build the houses at a given distance from the street, contributes to its beauty, it produces a disgusting monotony, all persons make this complaint against Philadelphia, the contrary practice varies the appearance, & is much much more convenient to the inhabitants. In Paris it is forbidden to build a house beyond a given height, & it is admitted to be a good restriction, it keeps houses low & convenient, & the streets light and airy, fires are much more managable where houses are low.[8]

With the characteristic thoroughness of a long-range planner, he foresaw almost every problem that would be encountered. As an experienced lawyer, he suggested "that the President inform himself of the several rival positions [of the Capitol]; leaving among them inducements to bid against each other in offers of land or money, as the location when completed by the survey will not be mutable by the President, it may be well to have the offers so framed as to become *ipso facto* absolute in favor of the U.S. on the event which they solicit." This advice became valuable in later disputes about changes in the adopted plan. He thought "The President [should] direct the Survey of the District which he shall ultimately elect. [And] it seems essential that the District should comprehend the water adjoining the establishment, and it should comprehend the opposite shore."[9] For this recommendation he recited the legal justification in the 1790 act. As a result, the District originally extended across the river into northern Virginia, including the town of Alexandria and parts of the neighboring counties (fig. 23).

With typical logic, Jefferson outlined the procedure for creating the capital.

The district being defined & the requisite quantity of ground secured, the next step must be to fix the site for the public buildings—and provide for the establishment or enlargement of a town within the district. . . . The plan for the public buildings is to be approved by the President. The Commissioners will no doubt submit different ones formed by themselves, or obtained

[8] Ibid., p. 31.
[9] Ibid., p. 32.

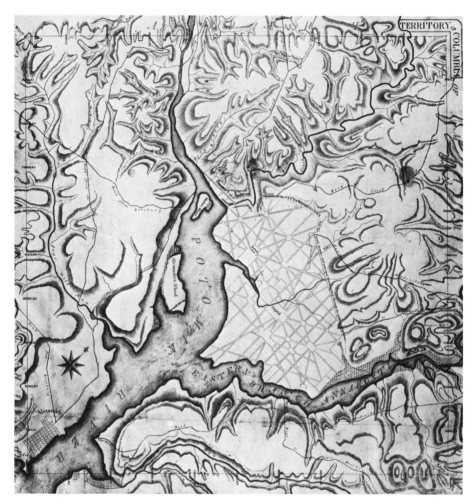

Fig. 23. District of Columbia boundaries, 1791, with L'Enfant plan superimposed (Library of Congress)

from ingenious architects. Should it be thought proper to excite emulation by a premium for the best, the expense is authorized, as an incident to that of the Buildings.

A competition had obviously been in Jefferson's mind from the first. But both he and the commissioners were constantly plagued with the fear that Congress would become impatient and change its mind and, "if the present occasion of securing the Federal seat on the Potowmack should be lost, it could never more be regained, that it would be dangerous to rely on any aids from Congress, or the assemblies of Virginia or Maryland, & that therefore measures should be adopted to carry the residence bill into execution without recourse to those bodies: and that the requisites were 1st land enough to place the buildings on; & 2ndly money enough to build them."[10]

In letters to Daniel Carroll, Thomas Johnson, and David Stuart in January 1791, Jefferson wrote: "The President of the united States desirous of availing your assistance in preparing the federal seat on the Potomac, has appointed you one of three Commissioners directed by the law for that purpose. . . . I have the honor to enclose you a copy of the Proclamation meant to constitute your first direction." The proclamation said, "The President, thinking it would be better that the outline, at least, of the city, and, perhaps Georgetown, should be laid down in the plat of the territory, I have the honor now to send it and to desire that Major Ellicott may do it as soon as convenient, that it may be returned in time to be laid before Congress."[11]

This proclamation makes clear the part Jefferson took in fixing the boundaries of the District before Major Charles Pierre L'Enfant[12] was brought into the picture. Two weeks later another letter to Johnson and Stuart said, "The President having thought Major L'Enfant peculiarly qualified to make such a draft of the ground as will enable himself to fix on the spot for the public buildings, he has written to for that purpose, and will be sent on if he chuses to undertake it." He must have accepted, because Jefferson wrote him in March 1791: "You are desired to proceed to Georgetown, where you will find Mr. Ellicot employed in making a survey and map of the Federal territory. The special object of asking your aid is to have drawings of the particular grounds most likely to be approved for the site of the federal town and buildings." Then followed specific instructions of how and where to proceed, ending with the request, "I

[10] Ibid., pp. 33–34.

[11] Ibid., pp. 37–38.

[12] Dos Passos, "Builders for a Golden Age," *American Heritage* 10, no. 5 (1959): 65–77.

will beg the favor of you to mark me your progress about twice a week, by letter."[13] By these very clear instructions, without dictating design, Major L'Enfant's function was explicitly outlined. This did not mean that the responsibility for producing an acceptable plan had been transferred from Jefferson to the genius from Versailles. Now he had the double responsibility of steering both the production and the producer of a plan that could be presented to the legislature.

L'Enfant encountered weather difficulties of which he said: "I shall be much at a loss how to make a plan of the ground you have pointed out to me and have it ready for the President at the time when he is expected at this place. . . . As far as I was able to judge through a thick fog I passed on many spots which appeared to me raly beautiful and which seem to dispute with each other who command."[14] He was searching for the best location for the Capitol.

At the same time he made the gesture of studying other city plans, as revealed by his letter to Jefferson from "jeorgetown, April the 4th. 1791":

I would be very much obliged to you . . . if you could procure for me what Ever may fall within your reach—of any of the different grand city now existing such as for example—as London—Madry [Madrid]—paris—Amsterdam—naples—venice—genoa—florence together with particular maps of any such sea ports or dock yards and arsenals . . . I would reprobate the Idea of Imitating and that contrary to Having this Intention it is my wish and shall be my Endeavour to delinate on a new and original way the plan the contrivance of which the President has left to me without any restriction soever."[15]

To this request Jefferson promptly replied:

I have examined my papers and found plans of Frankfort on the Mayne, Carlsruhe, Amsterdam, Strasburg, Paris, Orleans, Bordeaux, Lyons, Montpelier, Marseilles, Turin and Milan [figs. 24–32], which I send in a roll by this Post. They are on large and accurate scales, having been procured by me while in those respective cities myself. As they are connected with the notes I made in my travels, and often necessary to explain them to myself, I will beg your care of them and to return them when no longer useful to you, leaving you absolutely free to keep them as long as useful. I am happy that

[13] Padover, pp. 39, 42, 43.
[14] Ibid., p. 46.
[15] Ibid., pp. 56–57.

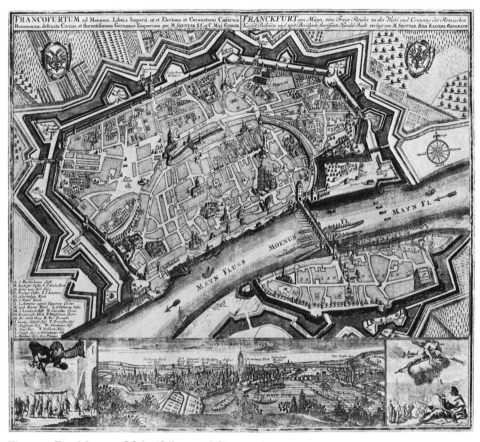

Fig. 24. Frankfurt am Main (Library of Congress)

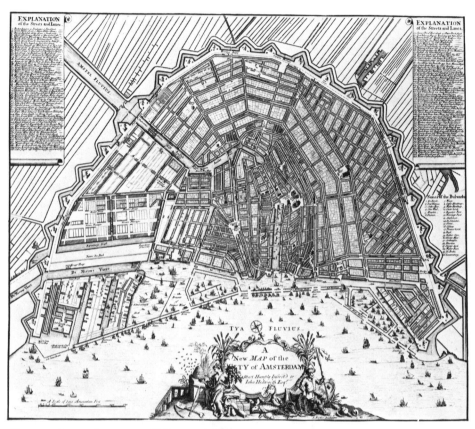

Fig. 25. Amsterdam, 1720 (Library of Congress)

Fig. 26. Strasbourg, 1734 (Library of Congress)

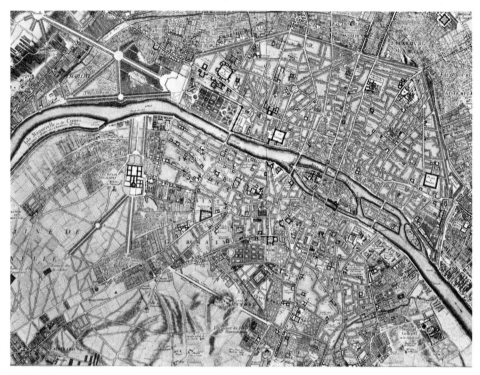

Fig. 27. Paris (Library of Congress)

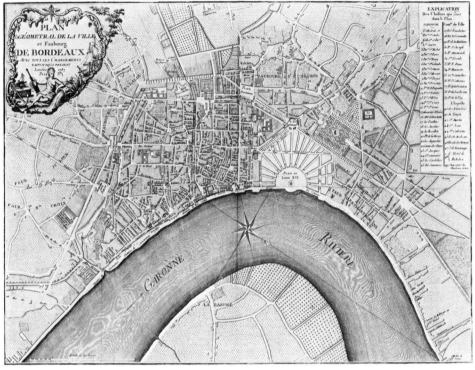

Fig. 28. Bordeaux, 1787 (Library of Congress)

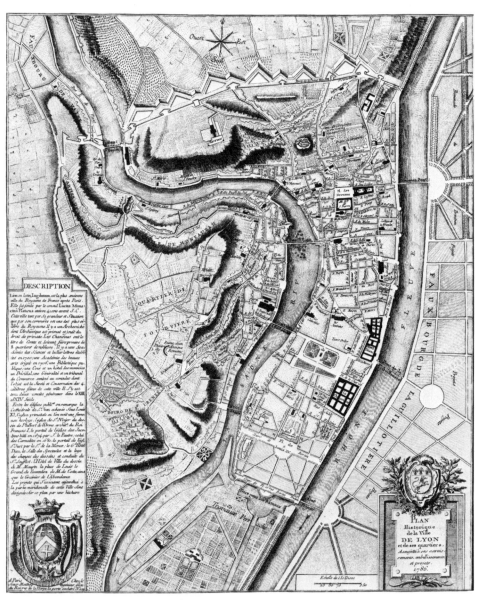

Fig. 29. Lyon, 1786 (Library of Congress)

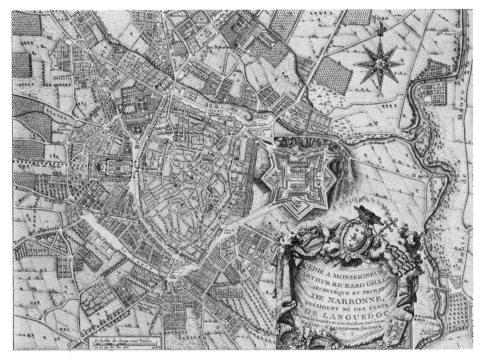

Fig. 30. Montpellier (Library of Congress)

Fig. 31. Turin (Library of Congress)

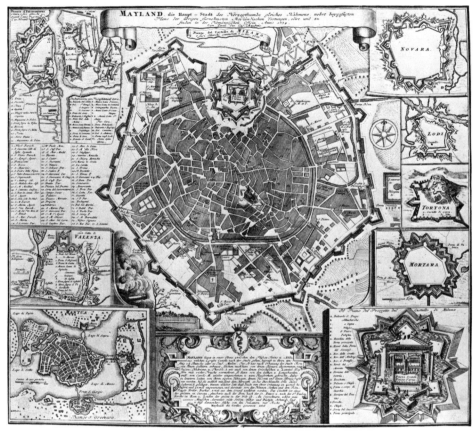

Fig. 32. Milan, 1734 (Library of Congress)

the President has left the planning of the Town in such good hands, and have no doubt it will be done to general satisfaction.[16]

In this same letter it is pertinent to note how Jefferson was trying to relinquish his own conception of the "town," as he persistently referred to what everyone else was calling the "city," in favor of the ideas that might emanate from Washington's newfound French designer: "Having communicated to the President, before he went away, such general ideas on the subject of the Town, as occurred to me, I make no doubt that, in explaining himself to you on the subject, he has interwoven with his own ideas, such of mine as he approved: for fear of repeating therefore, what he did not approve, and having more confidence in the unbiassed state of his mind, than in my own, I avoid interfering with what he may have expressed to you." Nevertheless, he could not resist adding, "Whenever it is proposed to prepare plans for the Capitol, I should prefer the adoption of some one of the models of antiquity, which have had the approbation of thousands of years." This was Jefferson's subtle but nonetheless persuasive statement of the theme that he envisioned for the design character of the Capitol. Today's city is a monument to this theme. Jefferson went on to name the French buildings, among which was his favorite Hôtel de Salm in Paris, that he approved for the style of the President's House. He followed up with a letter to Washington: "While in Europe I selected about a dozen or two of the handsomest fronts of private buildings [of French classicism] of which I have the plates. perhaps it might decide the taste of the new town, were these to be engraved here, and distributed gratis among the inhabitants of Georgetown. the expence would be trifling."[17] Subtle coercion, this might be called; but that it was effective is apparent throughout the city.

What use, if any, L'Enfant made of "any of the different grand city now existing" whose plans he borrowed from Jefferson cannot be detected in the plan he produced. The scheme that L'Enfant submitted, despite his statement that "I would reprobate the idea of Imitating," was none other than André Le Nôtre's design for King Louis XIV's royal gardens of Versailles (figs. 33–34). No acknowledgment

---

[16] Ibid., pp. 58–59.
[17] Ibid., pp. 58–59., 60.

of Le Nôtre's design was offered.[18] No influential person, however, except perhaps John Adams and Jefferson, would have been sufficiently familiar with Versailles to have detected L'Enfant's adaptation.[19] If Jefferson recognized the source he said nothing because he appreciated the grandeur of the plan as conforming to his own philosophy of following the taste that had stood the test of time. Even though Versailles was by no means a thousand years old, it was the perfection of an art as old as civilization, and what's more, it fitted very well on the banks of the Potomac, and Washington liked it.

Jefferson was primarily interested in getting an acceptable plan. Like the pendulum of a clock he had been ticking off the hours pending the hour of that great decision. The L'Enfant plan brought the hour to strike, and the sound of approval, even though preliminary, was the sound Jefferson had longed to hear.

Fiske Kimball has explained:

L'Enfant's first draught of his plan for the city, August [1791; fig. 35] which seems to have already conformed in its general lines to his later drawings and the plan as executed . . . made a compromise with Jefferson's ideas, a compromise which resulted in the unique plan adopted for the city. The radial plan was superimposed on the rectangular, at the same time preserving the general arrangement of the main elements which Jefferson had suggested. L'Enfant's draught, with small alterations, Washington accepted, and showed to the property owners on June 30 as substantially the design to be executed. Jefferson this time was not at hand to be consulted, and did not see the plan until L'Enfant brought his revised draught to Philadelphia toward the end of August, when, after a conference with his lieutenants there, Washington gave his approval. Though it is not sure Jefferson considered the radial avenues wholly as improvements, he certainly acquiesced in the adoption of the plan, and supported it afterwards with unswerving loyalty.[20]

From this account it is clear that Kimball, the greatest authority on Jefferson's architectural accomplishments, gave him, along with L'Enfant, almost equal credit for the plan of Washington. With an approved plan in hand, it was the secretary of state's responsibility to get it laid out on the ground and raise the money to get the public

[18] Fiske Kimball, *American Architecture* (Indianapolis, 1928), p. 78.
[19] Franklin had died the year before.
[20] Kimball, *Thomas Jefferson, Architect*, p. 51.

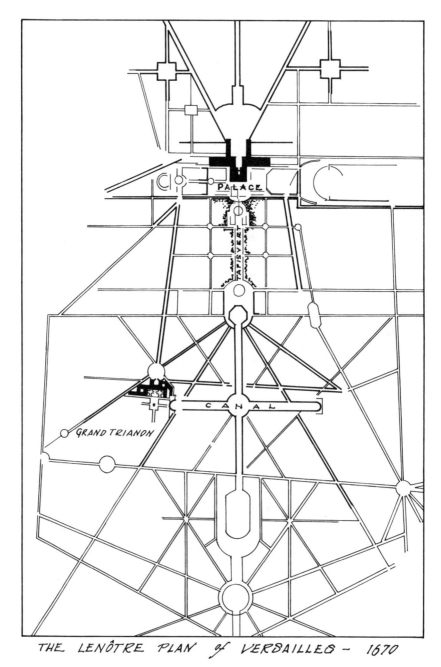

THE LENÔTRE PLAN of VERSAILLES – 1670

Fig. 33. Diagram showing plan of Versailles (sketched by Ralph Griswold). Compare with fig. 34.

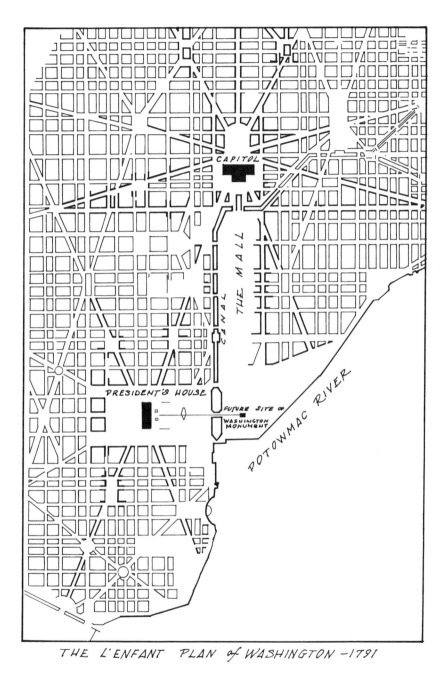

THE L'ENFANT PLAN of WASHINGTON –1791

Fig. 34. Diagram showing Washington (sketched by Ralph Griswold). Compare with fig 33.

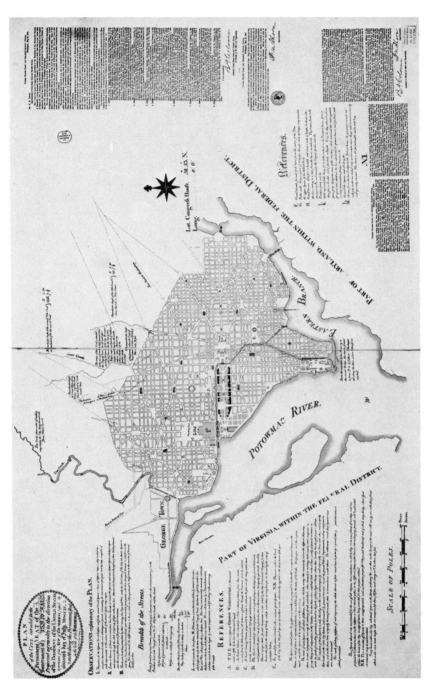

Fig. 35. L'Enfant plan of Washington, D.C., 1791, as redrawn in 1887 (Library of Congress)

buildings designed and constructed. His troubles began with L'Enfant. For the Capitol, although Jefferson had definite ideas he had
sketched (fig. 36), he knew that the president hoped to obtain a
design from L'Enfant.[21] But before he put anything on paper, this
temperamental Frenchman had not only ruined his chances of designing the Capitol but also destroyed his opportunity to supervise
the construction of his plan for the city. Apparently he overestimated
his influence with Washington when, on the pretext that Commissioner Carroll's house interfered with the execution of his plan, he
tore it down. This stupid miscalculation of his authority, or, as some
thought, his "private resentment against Mr. Carroll," had finally to
be referred to the president, who backed Jefferson and the commissioners. Upon notification that he was to "be in subordination to the
Commissioners," L'Enfant replied, "I cannot nor would I upon any
consideration submit myself to it." By this arrogance he lost the
support of Washington, who regretfully instructed Jefferson that if
L'Enfant remained adamant in his stand, his services were to be
terminated. This Jefferson did on February 27, 1792, in a letter to
L'Enfant saying: "From your letter received yesterday . . . it is
understood that you absolutely decline acting under the authority of
the present Commissioners. If this understanding of your meaning
be right I am instructed by the President to inform you that not-
withstanding the desire he has entertained to preserve your agency in
the business the condition upon which it is to be done is inadmis-
sable, & your services must be at an end."[22] Having been given every
consideration in polite language, L'Enfant held, nevertheless, to his
stubborn attitude, and as a result was fired. Jefferson was left with
the responsibility for completing a plan that was only in its preliminary stage and required many interpretations and revisions. Without
his sympathetic implementation the L'Enfant plan would probably
never have been carried out.

According to the secretary's self-imposed code of ethics L'Enfant
had committed the unforgivable sin—he had been disloyal to President Washington, the man who had been instrumental in appointing
him. To all the cries of unfair treatment that were subsequently
addressed to the secretary, he replied with courteous but strictly legal

[21] Ibid., p. 52.
[22] Padover, pp. 78, 99, 100.

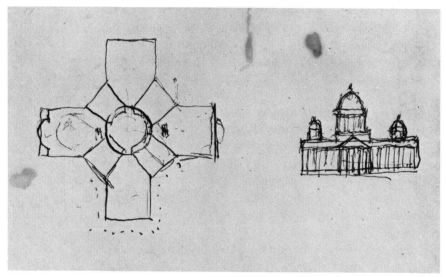

Fig. 36. Study for the design of the Capitol by Jefferson (Massachusetts Historical Society)

interpretation. With the approved plan that located the Capitol and President's House to work with, Jefferson's next job was to get these buildings built in time for the legislature's occupancy in the year 1800 at the proposed termination of their temperary seat in Philadelphia. Without knowing how much more time he was to be in a position of authority, the secretary exerted himself to get these buildings completed and the L'Enfant plan laid out. For the first task he promoted a competition which occupied much of his time but was not primarily concerned with his ability as a landscape architect. Until L'Enfant's plan was laid out on the ground, lots could not be sold, money could not be raised, and buildings, no matter how beautifully designed, could not be built. The task of transferring the approved plan from paper to the site was entrusted to Andrew Ellicott, the surveyor who had already been engaged to lay out the boundaries of the District. With his skill as a surveyor, Ellicott redrew L'Enfant's plan with greater precision and detail without altering the design. In this plan, like its predecessors, the axes of the Capitol and President's House intersected on the Potomac waterfront, then at the approximate location of what later became the site of the Washington Monument (fig. 37). An open view of the river from both buildings must have been intended at that time. The Tyber River (variously called Goose Creek or Hunting Creek) had been filled in and the canal, as Jefferson wanted it,[23] extended parallel to the mall to a point west of the Capitol and thence across town to the Eastern Branch (Anacostia River).

It seems certain that Jefferson had his eye on this focal point on the riverfront for an equestrian statue of General Washington that he tried to promote through the commissioners. To them, he had recommended the sale of enough lots to enable them to employ

Mr. Ceracchi, the artist, who had proposed to execute the monument. . . . he is unquestionably an artist of the first Class. he has had the advantage of taking the model of the President's person in plaster, equal to every wish in resemblance and Spirit, it is Pretty certain, that the Equestrian Statue of the President can never be executed by an equal workman, who has had equal advantages, and the Question is, whether a prudent caution will permit you to enter into any engagement, now taking time enough before the term of payment, to have accomplished the more material objects of the public buildings &c.[24]

He outlined the terms of payment practically endorsing Ceracchi's employment. But the commissioners exercised more "prudent caution" than he anticipated by replying: "We are of Oppinion that in the application of the Funds, we ought to class our work, into Necessary, Useful, and Ornamental, preferring them in that order. Without going into the Question of right to apply the money to defray the expence of Mr. Cerachie's Design or the propriety of the design itself, we decline going into that business."[25] Jefferson was defeated by his own cautious procedure, and General Washington was eventually commemorated by a gigantic pagan obelisk instead of an equestrian statue silhouetted against the river he loved so well. Whether Jefferson's taste or that of his planning successors was preferable is a moot question.

Preoccupied as he had been with getting the building program under way, Jefferson did not have time to do what he probably

[23] Ibid., p. 267.
[24] Ibid., p. 133.
[25] Ibid., p. 135.

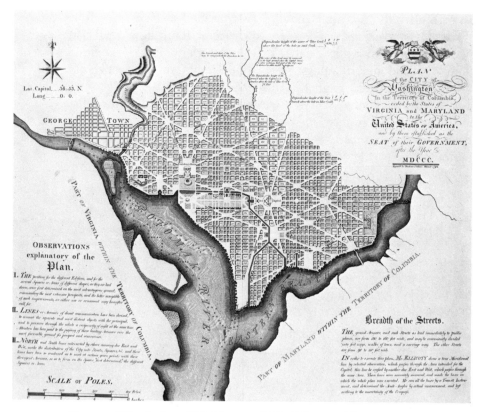

Fig. 37. Ellicott plan of Washington, D.C. (Library of Congress)

intended about the streets and waterfront when he first studied the site. When he became president of the United States, Jefferson went into action on the street plan and, on October 13, 1801, according to a note of the commissioners, "communicated personally with the Board at their office on the Affairs of the City, directed that the Streets from the President's Square to the Upper Bridge over Rock Creek; and New Jersey Avenue from the Bridge to the Capitol shall be compleated, Pennsylvania Avenue first done—the footways in, & adjacent to, the Capitol Square repair'd: & a footway made to the South side of the President's Enclosure."[26] Jefferson practically

[26] Ibid., p. 232.

became "clerk of the works" for the development of the capital.

On December 4, 1801, the commissioners issued a memorial to the president including in part "An enumeration of the houses in the City of Washington, made November, 1801." According to this table of "Houses in a habitable state on the 15th May, 1800," there were 109 of "Brick" and 163 of "Wood."[27] This was also the date of the Ellicott revised official plan of the city. There was a vast open space at the time of this report betwen completed houses and the projected plan to be filled by the president.

In June 1802, when the term of office of the Commissioners expired, they left "the Books Plans Papers Instruments and other articles . . . in the custody of Mr. Munroe our Clerk, to be delivered to the Superintendent when appointed by the President." As if this was not enough responsibility, he also appointed Robert Brent to be "Mayor of the . . . City of Washington," "in pursuance of the powers vested in me by the Act of Congress."[28] The act cited as his authority for this appointment used the term "District of Columbia" instead of "Territory of Columbia" as previously agreed upon by the commissioners. Why this change was made is not recorded, but the new name has persisted.

The new mayor was given the responsibility of constructing the jail, but when he had trouble with the installation of the bars in the windows he received detailed instructions from the president telling him how to solve his problem. In gratitude for this favor, the mayor wrote a somewhat ambiguous letter, "Sir, the new jail is now ready for your reception."[29]

Thomas Munroe, in whose hands the affairs of the commissioners had been left, called the president's attention to the necessity for appointing Nicholas King as surveyor, and he did this in August 1802. King's services, highly valuable for laying out lots and streets, were directed by proclamation from the president. For instance, in answer to a request by the "Citizens and House holders in that part of the City of Washington which lies west of the President's house," he declared "that the said open space be, and the same hereby is appropriated and granted as a site for a Market."[30]

[27] Ibid., pp. 245–52.
[28] Ibid., pp. 270, 271.
[29] Ibid., p. 292.
[30] Ibid., p. 283.

In his anxiety to have the essential buildings and streets ready for Congress, Jefferson left the raison d'être of his original site location, the Potomac River, undeveloped. L'Enfant's plan for this most important area was vague. Ellicott's official recorded plan was also inadequate. Apparently, the commissioners had adopted a waterfront plan in 1795 and instructed Nicholas King to lay it out. But it was eleven years later, 1806, when he was directly responsible to the president, that he revealed its details. Since these waterfront plans were all drastically changed later, they are now significant only for their record of early environmental and water pollution control. King's letter to Jefferson in 1806 states:

Perfecting this part of the plan, so as to leave nothing for conjecture, litigation, or doubt, in the manner which shall most accord with the published plans, secure the health of the city, and afford the most general convenience to the merchants, requires immediate attention. . . .

The principle adopted in the engraved plan, if carried into effect and finally established in the plan now laid out upon the ground, when aided by proper regulations as to the materials and mode of constructing wharves for vessels to lay at and discharge their cargoes on, seems well calculated to preserve the purity of the air.[31]

His proposed water street would

form a general communication between the wharves and warehouses of the different merchants; and, by facilitating intercourses, render a greater service to them than they would derive from a permission to wharf and build at pleasure. The position of this Water street being determined, it will ascertain the extent and situation of the building squares and streets on the made ground, from the bank of the river, and bring the present as near to the published plan as now can be done. . . .

Along the water side of this street the free current or stream of the river should be permitted to flow, and carry with it whatever may have been brought from the city along the streets or sewers. . . . it would seem proper to prohibit the erection of houses, or anything obstructing a free circulation of air. . . .

. . . If it is not done at this time the evils will increase and every year add to our difficulties.[32]

Prevention of stream pollution had not yet advanced to the point

[31] Ibid., pp. 316–18.
[32] Ibid., pp. 318–20.

where downstream towns were protected from upstream pollution, but fortunately there were few towns on the lower reaches of the Potomac. The care taken to prevent stream and air pollution in the District was very advanced. That Jefferson intended the riverfront for commercial wharfage everywhere except at the terminals of the main axes is indicated in all the early plans. Waterfronts had not yet come into use for recreational or ornamental purposes. That concept was too visionary when there were very few houses and no paved streets. But the streets were next in line for attention.

A stroke of good fortune came to Jefferson's aid in 1803 when he appointed Benjamin Henry Latrobe as surveyor of the public buildings.[33] At that time appropriations to be applied to the public buildings were under the direction of President Jefferson, who wrote Latrobe: "This falls, of course, under the immediate business of the superintendent, Mr. Munroe, whose office is substituted for that of the board of commissioners. The former post of surveyor of the public buildings, which Mr. Hoban held until the dissolution of the board . . . ,will be revived. If you choose to accept it, you will be appointed to it, and would be expected to come on by the 1st of April."[34] For the first time Jefferson was to have a professionally trained architect as his assistant. Although he relied heavily on Latrobe's judgment, he never relinquished his prerogative as final arbiter on design.

The problem of planting trees on Pennsylvania Avenue was presented by Munroe to Jefferson with the same reliance on the president's opinion about landscaping as was placed on his handling of architectural problems.

We are proceeding with diligence in our operations on Pennsylvania Avenue according to your directions. It seems to be very general opinion here that without the trees are boxed, or otherwise protected from the horses and cattle a great many, if not all of them will be barked and destroyed—several instances have been pointed out to me where they were planted last year, and all destroyed.

[33] Benjamin Henry Latrobe (1764–1820), born in Yorkshire, Eng., was of French Huguenot ancestry and had been in this country since 1796. According to Talbot Hamlin, *Greek Revival Architecture in America* (1944; rept. New York, 1964), p. 33, "it is probably in the Capitol that we get the climax of Latrobe's work."

[34] Padover, p. 296.

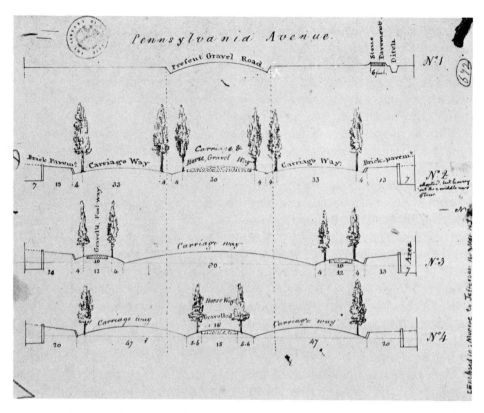

Fig. 38. Planting sketch for Pennsylvania Avenue, Washington, D.C., Munroe to Jefferson, 1803 (Library of Congress)

. . . Do you, Sir, think that a coat of whitewash, which I am told they give to the young trees in English Deer Parks would have any good effect? . . .

Dr. Thornton, Mr. King and myself have conversed on the manner of laying off the lines and planting the trees—The three modes illustrated by the enclosed sections [fig. 38]—were suggested—I mentioned the plan No. 3 as the one which I believed you had designed . . . —I shall get the trees from Mount Vernon, and Genl Masons Island . . . price twelve & a half Cents each.[35]

This was not exactly a "summit" problem, but Jefferson answered

[35] Ibid., pp. 297–98.

it as if it were: "No. 2 in the draught mr. King was so kind as to send me is exactly what Dr. Thornton explained to me as the original design except that he did not mention the two middle rows of trees but only the two outer ones on each side, and, omitting the two middle rows, I think this the best design. . . . it will allow us also next autumn . . . to plant our oaks, elms &c in the same lines with the lombardy poplars, giving to these trees of large growth a distance suitable to their size" (fig. 39). This fourth-dimensional thinking for future growth was followed by exact dimensions for planting.[36] His directions were as professional as those any landscape architect would give a contractor to perform this work.

Jefferson answered a problem brought up in 1804 by Nicholas King about property owners' rights in the layout of the lots in the vicinity of the White House in a way that clarified the status of the L'Enfant plan: "I think Mr. Davidson's error proceeds entirely from his considering L'Enfant's draught as the first plan; whereas it was only the first proposition prepared for, & subject to, future modifications. . . . I state these [conditions] only as my reasons for concurring with Genl. Washington in his decision of Feb. 97, a copy of which I will pray you to send Mr. Davidson."[37]

Latrobe proved himself to be not only competent but extremely tactful. In a letter asking about Italian stonecutters, he complimented Philip Mazzei on his importation of "vines" and "olives" to Virginia and requested, "Let us also owe to your kindness the introduction of excellence in the most fascinating branch of art."[38] Jefferson and Latrobe developed the "American Orders" which consisted of capitals enriched with flowers of tobacco or ears of corn, used in the small rotundas of the Capitol.

In 1805 Jefferson answered his grandaughter Ellen's inquiry as to whether gardening was an art: "To answer the question in your letter of the 4th. I must observe that neither the *number* of the fine arts nor the particular arts entitled to that appellation have been fixed by general consent. many reckon but five Painting, sculpture, architecture, music & poetry. . . . others again, add Gardening as a . . . fine art. not horticulture, but the art of embellishing grounds by fancy."[39]

[36] Ibid., p. 300.
[37] Ibid., p. 346.
[38] Ibid., p. 358.
[39] Betts, *Thomas Jefferson's Garden Book*, pp. 303–4.

Fig. 39. Washington, early view showing Lombardy poplars on Pennsylvania Avenue (Library of Congress)

In this definition there is the same basic thinking as that of the American Academy in Rome when in 1915 they recognized landscape architecture as a fine art by establishing a fellowship in that art along with architecture, painting, and sculpture. They were merely confirming Jefferson's opinion expressed one hundred years earlier.

Writing a note in great earnestness about the topping of trees and when it could be done with safety, with a recital of opinions pro and con, Thomas Munroe ended up by asking "the Opinion of the President whose experience & knowledge of these things he presumes enable him to say with certainty whether there ought to be a doubt entertained about "pruning in mid-May. Briefly and with "certainty" the president answered, "I think they may safely proceed."[40]

Of all things, Jefferson was elected to the City Council as a trustee for the public schools to be established in Washington and, supposedly to their amazement, accepted with a very gracious letter saying, "Sincerely believing that knowledge promotes the happiness of man, I shall ever be disposed to contribute my endeavors towards its extension; and, in the instance under consideration will willingly undertake the duties proposed to me."[41] Surely this is the only case in the history of this country where the president also served on the local school board. Jefferson had his own theories about public education and those who are fit to benefit by it; so, as usual, he did not consider himself too busy to put his theories into practice.

It was not until the attorney general rendered his opinion in 1806 regarding Samuel Davidson's claim that the official status of the L'Enfant and Ellicott plans was determined. In part of his opinion read:

In December following [Washington] communicated to them [Congress] the plan of L'Enfant, and after time given for its inspection, he withdrew it. This communication of the plan was intended merely as a matter of information, and to show in what state the business then was. All his subsequent acts and declarations conclusively prove that this plan had not then received his sanction. Major L'Enfant having been dismissed, Major Ellicott was in 1792 employed to prepare a plan, which he accordingly did; and although the ground work of the plan was the design of L'Enfant, yet President

[40] Padover, pp. 360–61.
[41] Ibid., p. 362.

Washington declares that many alterations deemed essential were made in it with his approbation, particularly in the public squares, which except those of the Capitol and President's House, were struck out of L'Enfant's design, and were left to future determination.[42]

That "future determination" was left largely to Jefferson. The "plan, thus compleated, was sent to Philadelphia to be engraved, was accordingly engraved, was promulgated throughout the United States, and, to use the expression of President Washington, was thereby intended to receive 'its final and regulating stamp.'"[43] There was no further ambiguity about the interpretation of L'Enfant's design.

The enclosure of vacant lots, "worn down with Indian corn," displeased the good farmer from Charlottesville: "therefore it was thought best as fast as the occupiers voluntarily withdrew their inclosures that they should not be reestablished, as the open grounds employed as a common in grass for the support of the cattle of the poor who depend much on them for subsistence are the more value to this City than inclosed and worn down with Indian corn."[44] Concern of this sort for the welfare of the poor in the development of the city was as deserving as the legal right of the proprietors.

A contrasting example of Latrobe's professional behavior compared with that of L'Enfant is shown in a letter of the highly skilled architect to Jefferson about the White House grounds.

I hope to accomplish your objects as respects the arrangement of the grounds around the President's house.

. . . I know well that *to you* it is my duty to obey implicitly or to resign my office: to myself it is my duty to maintain myself in a situation in which I can provide for my family by all honorable means. If in any instance my duty to you obliged me to act contrary to my judgment. I might fairly and honorably say with Shakespeare's apothecary: "My poverty, not my will consents." Such excuse, however, I have never wanted, . . . no mercenary motive whatever has kept me at my post, but considerations very superior to money—the attachment arising from gratitude and the highest esteem.[45]

Except for this difference in professional attitude, L'Enfant instead of

[42] Ibid., p. 367.
[43] Ibid., pp. 366–67.
[44] Ibid., p. 365.
[45] Ibid., pp. 389–90.

Latrobe might have been the one who supervised the Capitol and President's House to their completion.

Two instances of self-restraint exemplify the financial caution with which Jefferson proceeded. With regard to the planting of Pennsylvania Avenue, one of his favorite projects, he told Munroe: "the funds will admit only to gravel it *where* it is wanting and *as much* only as is necessary to make it firm. the planting with oaks et. & additional arch to the bridge must be abandoned." How closely Jefferson and Latrobe worked on the White House grounds is indicated by a Latrobe letter of April 29, 1807, which seems to describe an unsigned drawing (fig. 40).[46] Again, regarding the President's House, Jefferson instructed Latrobe:

Let the other half of the wall [around the grounds] be immediately begun, & be raised one foot higher than what is already done, & that which is already done be raised one foot higher, & the capping then to be put on as far as it is already prepared. no Gate or lodge to be attempted till we see the state of our funds at the finishing of the wall so far. when this is done so far, let us begin the stone steps, & when they are finished, and money enough put by for planting the grounds we will consider how best to employ what may remain on capping & Gates. so that the order of this part of the work is to be 1st. the wall completed and raised— 2. the steps—3. planting—4. capping, Gates, Porter's lodge, doing one at a time, finishing, settling & paying off one article before we begin another.[47]

Important as it was to that great "embellisher of Grounds by Fancy," planting had to take its place behind financial integrity.

There was no relaxation of responsibility even though there remained only one more year before he intended to retire to Monticello. Latrobe's report to Congress in 1808 enabled the president, in his letter of transmittal, to say that "the wall of inclosure round the Presidents Ground has been completed & the workmen are now setting the coping. A flight of stone steps, a bridge [the grounds then terminated on the banks of the Tyber], & platform, over the area of the North front are nearly completed. The appropriated [*sic*] being now nearly exhausted the work must soon be closed."[48]

Without the necessity of a professional code of ethics, Jefferson

[46] Ibid., pp. 393, 387–88.
[47] Ibid., p. 414.
[48] Ibid., pp. 445–48.

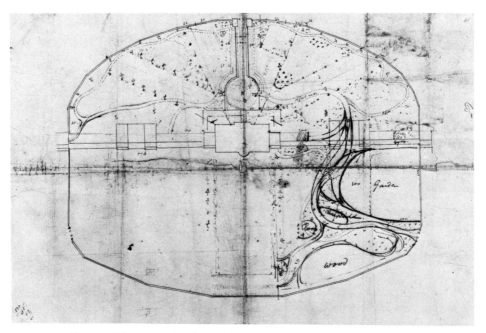

Fig. 40. Sketch plan for the revision of the White House grounds. Listed as "author unknown" by the Library of Congress, but Latrobe's letter to Jefferson, April 29, 1807, would seem to identify Benjamin Henry Latrobe as its designer (Library of Congress)

created one for himself that may well be emulated by all professional artists. In appreciation of his services, upon his retirement from the presidency in March 1809, a committee of Washington citizens addressed a letter to him.

To you they have been instructed to ascribe the memorable act, which, by declaring a gallant people free and independent, in a tone that appalled tyranny, instilled those sentiments and principles, which, inspiring every virtue, and urging every sacrifice, led them to triumph and empire.

We have since beheld you with parental solicitude, and with a vigilance that never sleeps, watching over the fairest offspring of liberty, and by your unremitted labors, in upholding, explaining and vindicating our system of government, rendering it the object of love at home and respect abroad. . . .

The world knows you as a philosopher and philanthropist; the American people know you as a patriot and statesman—we know you in addition to all this as a *man*.[49]

These sentiments, though expressed in language more flowery than his own taste, must have been welcome consolation for the vilification Jefferson had suffered from his political enemies during his presidential campaigns. His acknowledgment of this farewell letter expresses sentiments pertinent to today's conditions.

That differences of opinion should rise among men, on politics, on religion, and on every topic of human inquiry, and that these should be freely expressed in a country where all our facilities are free is to be expected. But these valuable privileges are much perverted when permitted to disturb the harmony of social intercourse, and to lessen the tolerance of opinion. To the honor of society here, it has been characterized by a just and generous liberality, and an indulgence of those affections which, without regard to political creeds, constitute the happiness of life. That the improvements of this city must proceed with sure and steady steps, following from its many obvious advantages, and from the enterprizing spirit of its inhabitants, which promises to render it the fairest seat of wealth and science.[50]

Back home at Monticello in 1809, Jefferson left the supervision of the capital in the hands of his friend Latrobe, to whom he addressed an invitation to visit him, saying:

it . . . will give me real pleasure and I think could not fail of giving some to you. my essay in Architecture has been so much subordinated to the law of convenience, & affected also by the circumstance of change in the original design, that it is liable to some unfavorable & just criticisms. but what nature has done for us is sublime & beautiful and unique. you could not fail to take out your pencil & to add another specimen of it's excellence in landscape to your drawing of the Capitol & Capitol hill.[51]

The city of Washington was still on his mind.

[49] Ibid., pp. 58–60.
[50] Ibid., pp. 460–61.
[51] Ibid., p. 463.

CHAPTER IV

Influence of
Landscape Garden Literature

As the marquis de Chastellux said when he visited Monticello in 1782, Jefferson had set his house, like his mind, on the heights.[1] His genius for imaginative site location was also apparent in the other houses he designed, such as Poplar Forest, and in Barboursville and Bremo, which he influenced. For these houses he could exploit the knowledge of landscape design he had acquired from his reading and observation. Many were the compromises he made to gain the advantage of a commanding site. On his mountaintop at Monticello he ran the risk of insufficient water, but the prospect of having to haul it or depend on leaky cisterns did not deter him from choosing an inspiring view.

In his own magnificent library were books whose authors excited his imagination with the best landscape descriptions of the ages. They included Robert Castell's *The Villas of the Ancients*, 1728, John James's translation of Dezallier d'Argentville's *The Theory and Practice of Gardening*, 1728, Sir William Chambers's *Views . . . at Kew*, 1763, Joseph Heely's *Letters on the Beauties of Hagley, Envil, and the Leasowes*, 1777, B. Seeley's *Stowe: A Description*, 1783, William Mason's *The English Garden*, 1768, and Thomas Whately's *Observations on Modern Gardening*, 1770.[2] From these Jefferson could visualize garden history like an astronaut viewing the earth. As is the case with all artists who have created something new and beautiful, he was consulted by his friends when they wanted to build new houses and gardens. He wrote to Robert Skipwith in 1771, citing three leading writers of the time that he would recommend for their books on aesthetics: William Hogarth, Lord Kames, and Edmund Burke.

[1] Marquis de Chastellux, *Travels in North America, in the Years 1780, 1781, and 1782*, ed. Howard C. Rice, Jr. (Chapel Hill, N.C., 1963), p. 392. Parts of this chapter are based on Eleanor Berman's *Thomas Jefferson Among the Arts* (New York, 1947).

[2] All of these books were published in London, except Seely's, which was published in Buckingham.

The serpentine curve was the basis for Hogarth's philosophy. Jefferson noted its beauty in his description of contour plowing, as well as his respect for natural forms: "The plough is to the farmer what the wand is to the sorcerer. . . . We now plough horizontally following the curvatures of the hills and hollows. . . . In point of beauty nothing can exceed that of the waving lines & rows winding along the face of the hills & vallies."[3] Sixty years earlier in *The Analysis of Beauty*, published in 1753, Hogarth had written in praise of combining the beautiful and the useful; a typical comment was: "In nature's machines how wonderfully do we see beauty and use go hand in hand." Hogarth described his line of beauty: "Among the vast variety of waving-lines that may be conceived, there is but one that truly deserves the name of the line of beauty, so there is only one precise serpentine-line that I call the line of grace."[4]

That Hogarth illustrated his point by referring to garden design was not lost on Jefferson in his study of English gardens. The former wrote, "The eye has . . . enjoyment in winding walls, and serpentine rivers, and all sorts of objects, whose forms, as we shall see hereafter, are composed principally of what I call the waving and serpentine lines." Jefferson frequently noted his own distaste for straight lines in gardens. At Stowe, he wrote, "the straight approach is very ill," and at Caversham, he said; "a straight, broad gravel walk passes before the front and parallel to it. . . . This straight walk has an ill effect."[5]

Jefferson also found the books of Lord Kames and Burke very sympathetic as they were both concerned with visual beauty. Lord Kames stated in his *Elements of Criticism*, 1762, that an object without intrinsic beauty might appear beautiful if it was also useful. He also discussed the importance of large objects and the delightful sensation made by elevated ones. He found pleasure in looking down on objects and in ascending and descending heights. Such thinking is evident in Jefferson's choice of a mountaintop for Monticello. As he wrote to Maria Cosway from Paris in 1786, "How sublime to look

[3] Betts, *Thomas Jefferson's Garden Book*, p. 509.
[4] William Hogarth, *The Analysis of Beauty* (1753: rept. ed. Joseph Burke, Oxford, 1955), pp. 86, 102. It was Hogarth's book which marked the beginning of rococo in the art of the eighteenth century. As Fiske Kimball pointed out in the *Creation of the Rococo* (Philadelphia, 1943), the English introduced the style to the world of Louis XV's France, and not the other way around, as has been promulgated by French critics.
[5] Hogarth, p. 181; Betts, *Thomas Jefferson's Garden Book*, pp. 113, 112.

down into the workhouse of nature, to see her clouds, hail, snow, rain, thunder, all fabricated at our feet! and the glorious sun, when rising as if out of a distant water, just gilding the tops of mountains, and giving life to all nature! "[6] It was this sublime emotion which the English garden designers sought to awaken in the creation of their greatest landscapes. Both Lord Kames and Jefferson saw garden design as an extension of the beauties of nature.

Burke, however, in his *Essay on the Sublime and the Beautiful*, 1756, introduced a new concept: "Whatever is fitted in any sort to excite the ideas of pain and danger, that is to say, whatever is in any sort terrible, or is conversant about terrible objects, or operates in a manner analogous to terror, is a source of the *sublime*; that is, it is productive of the strongest emotion which the mind is capable of feeling." It was this feeling of terror which Jefferson described when he visited the Natural Bridge: it is "the most sublime of Nature's works. . . . You involuntarily fall on your hands and feet, creep to the parapet and peer over it. Looking down from this height about a minute, gave me a violent head ach." But, he went on reassuringly, "if the view from the top be painful and intolerable, that from below is delightful in an equal extreme."[7]

Karl Lehman has called Jefferson the greatest classicist of his time in America, and we know that he was able to read Greek and Latin "with his feet on the fender." Homer, whom he admired, described the gardens of Alcinous. Jefferson regarded himself as an Epicurean, and that philosopher taught in a garden in Athens. Pliny described both city houses and country villas, and Virgil extolled the delights of country life in his *Georgics*. Once Jefferson got to Italy, in the 1780s, he found that lack of time forced him to postpone a visit to Vicenza to see the villas of Palladio (fig. 41), with which he was so familiar through his books. The same reason prevented a trip to Rome. He never managed to make another tour of Italy.

When only twenty-one, Jefferson had bought *James on Gardening*, 1728, a translation of A. J. Desallier d'Argentville's book on the formal, aristocratic type of French gardens that Le Nôtre had designed at Vaux le Vicomte and at Versailles. But once in France,

[6] Lipscomb and Bergh, V: 436–37.

[7] Edmund Burke, *Essay on the Sublime and the Beautiful* (rept. Oxford, 1925), p. 91: Jefferson, *Notes on the State of Virginia*, pp. 24–25, 263.

Fig. 41. Villa Rotunda by Palladio, model from Vicenza in Dome Room of Rotunda at University of Virginia (University of Virginia Graphic Communications Services, Dan Grogan, photographer)

Jefferson heartily disliked Versailles with its rigid gardens expressive of the absolute monarchy of Louis XIV (fig. 42). However, the formal French style of the Sun King's favorite landscape architect, Le Nôtre, was popular in England in the seventeenth century. Not until the middle of the next century did the influence of Hogarth introduce the informal, or rococo, garden in England. Somewhat later it was introduced into France, where it became fashionable as the *jardin anglais*. The elegance of French neoclassical architecture, set in the naturalistic garden style of the English, appealed to Jefferson's mature taste.

At the age of twenty-two, in 1765, Jefferson had purchased

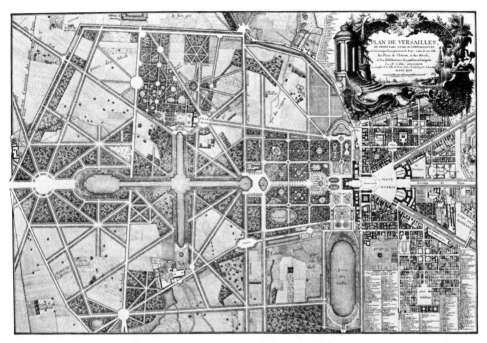

Fig. 42. Plan of Versailles, 1746 (Library of Congress)

William Shenstone's *Works*, published first in 1764. Shenstone was the first actually to describe the *jardin anglais* and its principles. At Leasowes, his home near Birmingham, he created a garden from a rocky unpromising site. Dr. Johnson wrote of this garden, saying that it should be visited by travelers and copied by designers.

Shenstone designed his garden as carefully as a painter composing a picture, explaining that "landskip should contain variety enough to form a picture upon canvas; and this is no bad test, as I think the landskip painter is the gardener's best designer." Jefferson felt the same way; he later tried to get George Parkyns, the landscape painter, to help him with Monticello's grounds. In summing up his theories of landscape design, Shenstone said: "Art, indeed, is often requisite to collect and epitomize the beauties of nature, but should never be suffered to set her mark upon them: I mean in regard to those articles that are of nature's province: the shaping of ground, the planting of trees, and the disposition of lakes and rivulets." Jefferson shared this view, for in writing about Blenheim, the great house in Oxfordshire, he said: "The garden has not great beauties. . . . the gravelled walks are broad—art appears too much."[8]

Such are the theories that Shenstone said he followed in laying out his estate. It is unfortunate that so little of his garden at Leasowes remains—it is now a golf course—and it is difficult to see how carefully he followed his own theories. Jefferson left us no adequate description of what he saw when he toured the place in 1786, but his notes show that he was not favorably impressed.

Leasowes, in Shropshire.—Now the property of Mr. Horne by purchase. One hundred and fifty acres within the walk. The waters small. This is not even an ornamented farm—it is only a grazing farm with a path round it, here and there a seat of board, rarely anything better. Architecture has contributed nothing. The obelisk is of brick. Shenstone had but three hundred pounds a year, and ruined himself by what he did to this farm. It is said that he died of the heartaches which his debts occasioned him. The part next the road is of red earth, that on the further part grey. The first and second cascades are beautiful. The landscape at number eighteen, and prospect at thirty-two, are fine. The walk through the wood is umbrageous and pleasing. The whole arch of prospect may be of ninety degrees. Many of the inscriptions are lost.[9]

Jefferson also learned a great deal about garden design from Thomas Whately's *Observations on Modern Gardening*. He owned the second edition of 1770. It was a well-organized work, setting forth both the principles of rococo naturalism in gardening and also detailed instructions on how to accomplish it.

When Jefferson and John Adams visited a group of famous gardens in the west of England in 1786, they took with them Whately's book. Jefferson tells us how he used it.

(Memorandum made on a tour to some of the gardens in England, described by Whateley in his book on Gardening.)

While his descriptions, in point of style, are models of perfect elegance and classical correctness, they are as remarkable for their exactness. I always walked over the gardens with his book in my hand, examined with attention the particular spots he described, found them so justly characterized by him

[8] William Shenstone, *Shenstone's Works*, 2 (later ed., London, 1773): 112–13, 126; Betts, *Thomas Jefferson's Garden Book*, p. 114.

[9] Betts, *Thomas Jefferson's Garden Book*, p. 113.

as to be easily recognized, and saw with wonder, that his fine imagination had never been able to seduce him from the truth. My inquiries were directed chiefly to such practical things as might enable me to estimate the expense of making and maintaining a garden in that style. My journey was in the months of March and April, 1786.[10]

Jefferson's own descriptions follow in this memorandum; they indicate his interest in the practical, as well as in the aesthetic. Curiously enough at Hagley he did not mention seeing in the garden the famous Greek revival temple by James Stuart, the first building of the style in England. He never liked the style, and that may perhaps explain his silence. Of Hagley, he said:

now Lord Wescot's.—One thousand acres: no distinction between park and garden—Both blended, but more of the character of garden. Eight or nine laborers keep it in order. Between two and three hundred deer in it, some of them red deer. They breed sometimes with the fallow. This garden occupying a descending hollow between the Clent and Witchbury hills, with the spurs from those hills, there is no level in it for a spacious water. There are, therefore, only some small ponds. From one of these there is a fine cascade; but it can only be occasionally, by opening the sluice. This is a small, dark, deep hollow, with recesses of stone in the banks on every side. In one of these is a Venus predique, turned half round as if inviting you with her into the recess. There is another cascade seen from the portico on the bridge. The castle is triangular, with a round tower at each angle, one only entire; it seems to be between forty and fifty feet high. The ponds yield a great deal of trout. The walks are scarcely gravelled.[11]

Jefferson did not always approve of Whately's descriptions of English estates, but he learned a great deal from them. In 1789 he wrote to Madame Broutin on July 13, saying that, as she had "un jardin Anglois," he was sending her Whately where "ce sujet est superieurement traité. A des principles tres fondes, l'Auteur ajoute des descriptions exactes et pittoresque des jardins les plus celebres de l'Angleterre." Whately's introduction describes the subject and ma-

---

[10] Ibid., pp. 111–14. Jefferson visited sixteen places between April 2 and 14, 1786: Chiswick, Hampton Court, Twickenham, Esther-Place, Claremont, Paynshill, Woburn, Caversham, Wotton, Stowe, Leasowes, Hagley, Blenheim, Enfield Chase, Moor Park, and Kew.

[11] Ibid., p. 113.

terials of landscape gardening in the best-organized book on the subject of its day:

Gardening, in the perfection to which it has been lately brought in England, is entitled to a place of considerable rank among the liberal arts. It is as superior to landskip painting, as a reality to a representation: it is an exertion of fancy, as subject for taste; and being released now from the restraints of regularity, and enlarged beyond the purposes of domestic convenience, the most beautiful, the most simple, the most noble scenes of nature are all within its province: for it is no longer confined to the spots from which it borrows its name, but regulates also the disposition and embellishments of a park, a farm, or a riding; the business of a gardener is to select and to apply whatever is great, elegant, or characteristic in any of them; to discover and to show all the advantages of the place upon which he is employed; to supply it defects, to correct its faults, and to improve the beauties.

Nature, always simple, employs but four materials in the composition of her scenes, *ground*, *wood*, *water*, and *rocks*. The cultivation of nature had introduced a fifth species, the *buildings* requisite for the accommodation of men. Each of these again admit of varieties in their figure, dimensions, colour, and situation. Every landskip is composed of these parts only; every beauty in a landskip depends on the applications of their several varieties.[12]

Of ground, Whately said, "The style of every part must be accommodated to the character of the whole; for every piece of ground is distinguished by certain properties."[13] This statement is consistent with Jefferson's general design principles.

Of wood, Whately wrote, after discussing the various types of trees and their arrangements, of the importance of perspective in landscape design. Jefferson was to discuss these ideas at length in a letter to William Hamilton in 1806. Whately described a painterly "effect: of a dark green tree, or groupe of trees, with nothing behind it but the splendor of a morning, or the glow of an evening sky, cannot be unknown to any who was ever delighted with a picture of Claude."[14]

Of water, Whately said that "it is always regretted when wanting."[15] Jefferson planned to use the springs at Monticello in a

---

[12] E. Millicent Sowerby, ed., *Catalogue of the Library of Thomas Jefferson* (Washington, D.C.: 1952–59), 4: 387; Whately, pp. 1–2.

[13] Whately, p. 13.

[14] Ibid., pp. 34–35.

[15] Ibid., p. 61.

decorative fashion, and seems to have believed that the lovely streams and rivers of North America, pristine and undefiled in his day, provided plenty of waterscapes without the necessity of creating them. He was struck with the rush of the waters at Harpers Ferry, which he regarded as a magnificent manifestation of nature.

After discussing many design details, Whately concluded with advice that is still of paramount importance today to landscape architects:

Whatever contributes to render the scenes of nature delightful, is amongst the subjects of gardening; and animate as well as inanimate objects, are circumstances of beauty or character . . . nothing is unworthy of the attention of a gardiner, which can tend to improve his compositions, whether by immediate effects, or by suggesting a train of pleasing ideas. The whole range of nature is open to him, from the parterre to the forest; and whatever is agreable to the senses or the imagination, he may appropriate to the spot he is to improve: it is part of his business to collect into one place, the delights which are generally dispersed through different species of country. . . .

The art of gardening therefore is not to be studied in those spots only where it has been exercised; though they are in this country very numerous, and very various . . . and unless the gardener has stored his mind with ideas, from the infinite variety of the country at large, he will feel the want of that number, which is necessary for choice. . . . But improved places are of singular use to direct the judgment in the choice, and the combinations of the beauties of nature: an extensive knowledge of them is to be acquired in the country where they casually occur; discernment of their excellencies, and a taste for the disposition of them, is to be formed in places where they have been selected, and arranged with design.[16]

Jefferson noted without comment the garden temples at Stowe, one of the most famous gardens in England and one that was considered the ideal. By 1755, the garden covered five hundred acres; Charles Bridgeman and William Kent worked here, and Sir John Vanbrugh designed some of the temples and monuments. Nevertheless, it did not appeal much to Jefferson:

Belongs to the Marquis of Buckingham. . . . Fifteen men and eighteen boys employed in keeping pleasure grounds. Within the walk are considerable portions separated by enclosures and used for pasture. . . . Kent's building is

[16] Ibid., pp. 256–57.

called the temple of Venus. The enclosure is entirely by ha-ha. At each end of the front line there is a recess like the bastion of a fort. In one of these is the temple of Friendship, in the other the temple of Venus. They are seen the one from the other, the line of sight passing, not through the garden, but through the country parallel to the line of the garden. This has a good effect. . . . The Corinthian arch has a very useless appearance, inasmuch as it has no pretension to any destination. Instead of being an object from the house, it is an obstacle to a very pleasing distant prospect. The Grecian valley being clear of trees, while the hill on each side is covered with them, is much deepened to appearance.[17]

Every eighteenth-century English garden with any claim to distinction had to have ruins, constructed in a scale and design to enhance a view. To Lord Kames ruins were meant to arouse "a sort of melancholy pleasure." Jefferson did not pay much attention to such ruins, or "follies," but he did like spirals in garden design (fig. 43), and he planned to use broom and other such shrubs to create them, suggesting: "The best way of forming thicket will be to plant it in labyrinth spirally, putting the tallest plants in the center & lowering gradation to the external termination. a temple, or a seat may be in the center . . . leaving space enough between the rows to walk & to trim up, replant, etc the shrubs."[18]

As with his training in architecture, Jefferson's skills in landscape were determined both by books and observation. While his volumes on landscape design in his library were not nearly as voluminous as those on architecture, nonetheless he used Whately's *Observations on Modern Gardening* not only as his guide and master in studying English gardens on the spot but as a reference once he returned to Virginia. He also owned two other books which contained good descriptions of great English landscape gardens: B. Seeley's *Stowe: A Description*, 1783, and Joseph Heely's *Letters on the Beauties of Hagley, Envil, and the Leasowes*, 1777. He could use both of these works to refresh his memories of these estates. But it was to Shenstone's *Works* in particular that he turned for inspiration in his landscape design for Monticello.

One book that he did not own and wrote to borrow unsuccessfully

[17] Betts, *Thomas Jefferson's Garden Book*, pp. 112–13.
[18] Henry Home, Lord Kames, *Elements of Criticism*, 2 (later ed., Edinburgh, 1774): 446–47; Kimball, *Thomas Jefferson, Architect*, p. 168, Plate 162.

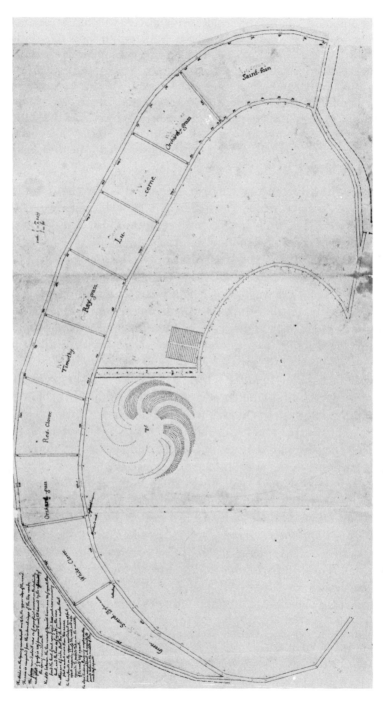

Fig. 43. Monticello, Jefferson's 1808 plan for laying off lots and making the mountainside a *ferme ornée* (The Huntington Library, San Marino, California)

was George Parkyns's *Six Designs*, 1793. Following the traditions of the day Parkyns was a painter as well as landscape gardener. He was able but obscure and would never have been rescued from oblivion but for his association with Jefferson. He may have met Parkyns in London in 1786 at the same time that he became acquainted with Richard and Maria Cosway, who were close friends of Sir John Soane, one of the leading English architects of the time. While Richard Cosway was busy making miniature paintings of his fasionable sitters, Maria and Jefferson explored Paris and Versailles and the gardens in the English fashion at Saint-Germain. A series of her letters to Soane and some of her landscape paintings are still in Soane's London house. Soane and Parkyns must also have had some association, since the latter's book was published as an appendix to Soane's *Sketches in Architecture*.[19]

Certain it is that by July 1806, Jefferson was influenced by Parkyns's work, for in a very appealing letter Jefferson invited the leading exponent of Parkyns's style in America, William Hamilton, to Monticello, to help him design his grounds like those of Hamilton's home, The Woodlands, near Philadelphia.

Having decisively made up my mind for retirement at the end of my present term [as president], my views and attentions are all turned homewards. I have hitherto been engaged in my buildings which will be finished in the course of the present year. The improvement of my grounds has been reserved for my occupation on my return home. For this reason it is that I have put off to the fall of the year after next the collection of such curious trees as will bear our winters in the open air.

The grounds which I destine to improve in the style of the English gardens are in a form very difficult to be managed. They compose the northern quadrant of a mountain for about ⅔ of its height & then spread for the upper third over its whole crown. They contain about three hundred acres, washed at the foot for about a mile, by a river of the size of the Schuylkill. The hill is generally too steep for direct ascent, but we make level walks successively along it's side, which in it's upper part encircle the hill & intersect these again by others of easy ascent in the various parts. They are chiefly still in their native woods, which are majestic, and very

[19] G. F. Parkyns, *Six Designs for Improving and Embellishing Grounds with Sections and Explanations*, (London, 1793), bound with John Soane's *Sketches in Architecture* . . . , copy at Dumbarton Oaks Garden Library, Washington, D.C.

generally a close undergrowth, which I have not suffered to be touched, knowing how much easier it is to cut away than to fill up. The upper third is chiefly open, but to the South is covered with a dense thicket of Scotch broom (Spartium scoparium Lin.) which being favorably spread before the sun will admit of advantageous arrangement for winter enjoyment. You are sensible that this disposition of the ground takes from me the first beauty in gardening, the variety of hill & dale, & leaves me as an awkward substitute a few hanging hollows & ridges, this subject is so unique and at the same time refractory, that to make a disposition analogous to its character would require much more of the genius of the landscape painter & gardener than I pretend to. I had once hoped to get Parkins to go and give me some outlines, but I was disappointed. Certainly I could never wish your health to be such as to render travelling necessary; but should a journey at any time promise improvement to it, there is no one on which you would be received with more pleasure than at Monticello. Should I be there you will have an opportunity of indulging on a new field some of the taste which has made the Woodlands the only rival which I have known in America to what may be seen in England.

Thither without doubt we are to go for models in this art. Their sunless climate has permitted them to adopt what is certainly a beauty of the very first order in landscape. Their canvas is of open ground, variegated with clumps of trees distributed with taste. They need no more of wood than will serve to embrace a lawn or a glade. But under the beaming, constant and almost vertical sun of Virginia, shade is our Elysium. In the absence of this no beauty of the eye can be enjoyed. This organ must yield it's gratification to that of the other senses; without the hope of any equivalent to the beauty relinquished. The only substitute I have been able to imagine is this. Let your ground be covered with trees of the loftiest stature. Trim up their bodies as high as the constitution & form of the tree will bear, but so as that their tops shall still unite & yield dense shade. A wood, so open below, will have nearly the appearance of open grounds. Then, when in the open ground you would plant a clump of trees, place a thicket of shrubs present-ing a hemisphere the crown of which shall distinctly show itself under the branches of the trees. This may be effected by a due selection & arrangement of the shrubs, & will I think offer a group not much inferior to that of trees. The thickets may be varied too by making some of them of evergreens altogether, our red cedar made to grow in a bush, evergreen privet, pyrocan-thus, Kalmia, Scotch broom. Holly would be elegant but it does not grow in my part of the country.

On prospect I have a rich profusion and offering itself at every point of the compass. Mountains distant & near, smooth & shaggy, single & in ridges, a little river hiding itself among the hills so as to shew in lagoons only, cultivated grounds under the eye and two small villages. To prevent a satiety of this is the principal difficulty. It may be successively offered, & in different portions through vistas, or which will be better, between thickets so disposed as to serve as vistas, with the advantage of shifting the scenes as you advance on your way.

You will be sensible by this time of the truth of my information that my views are turned so steadfastly homeward that the subject runs away with me whenever I get on it. I sat down to thank you for kindnesses received, & to bespeak permission to ask further contributions from your collection & I have written you a treatise on gardening generally, in which art lessons would come with more justice from you to me.[20]

William Birch, a well-known Philadelphia artist, indicated in his autobiography that Parkyns may have designed Hamilton's Woodlands along with James Greenleaf's estate Solitude in Fairmount Park, which he described as a "very engaging spot of much beauty." Jefferson seems also to have been influenced by Parkyns when he made suggestions to Latrobe about the plan for the White House grounds in 1807. There was a semicircular garden with a clump of trees, a wood, and a serpentine walk, all rather like those at Monticello.[21]

Although Jefferson had many of the important books on English landscape gardening, he did not have those of the well-known landscape gardeners Uvedale Price and Humphrey Repton and never mentioned their work. While Jefferson never pretended to be a landscape gardener, he was nonetheless the nearest equivalent to a landscape architect in the current fashion of early America. It was, however, not until the appearance of Alexander Jackson Downing, many years later, that the New World was to have a skillful designer in the landscape field, professionally identified as a landscape gardener.

[20] Betts, *Thomas Jefferson's Garden Book*, pp. 323–24.
[21] Eleanor McPeck, "George Isham Parkyns," *Quarterly Journal of the Library of Congress* 30 (July 1973): 171–82.

CHAPTER V

Monticello and Other Plantations

Monticello survives as one of the earliest and best-preserved examples of the English-type landscape gardens in America. The marquis de Chastellux described in 1782 a "garden laid out in the English style" at an estate in eastern Virginia on the Pamunkey River, but it presumably did not long outlast its owner, Thomas Jones, who died in 1786.[1] In other Jeffersonian gardens little else survives except the sites, drives, walls, some walks, and terraces. But because of many documents, mostly letters, sketches, and his Garden Book, it is known precisely what Jefferson planned and what he finally executed at Monticello (figs. 44–46).

In a wonderful letter to Charles Willson Peale in 1811, Jefferson revealed the high calling he believed the gardener's career to be, and pointed out that to him the cultivation of a garden was the most desirable of all professions: "No occupation is so delightful to me as the culture of the earth, and no culture comparable to that of the garden. . . . But though an old man, I am but a young gardener. . . . I have often thought that if heaven had given me a choice of my position and calling, it should have been on a rich spot of earth, well watered and near a good market for the production of the garden."[2] In 1771 Jefferson "set down elaborate plans for the development of the grounds at Monticello at the end of his Account Book rather than in his Garden Book." The plans begin:

choose out for a burying place some unfrequented vale in the park, where is "no sound to break the stillness but a brook, that bubbling winds among the weeds; no mark of any human shape that had been there, unless the skeleton of some poor wretch, Who sought that place out to despair and die in." let it be among antient and venerable oaks; intersperse some gloomy evergreens. the area circular, abt. 60 f. diameter, encircled with an untrimmed hedge of cedar, or of stone wall with a holly hedge on it in the form below. [Jefferson

---

[1] Chastellux, pp. 380, 569.
[2] Lipscomb and Bergh, 13: 78–79.

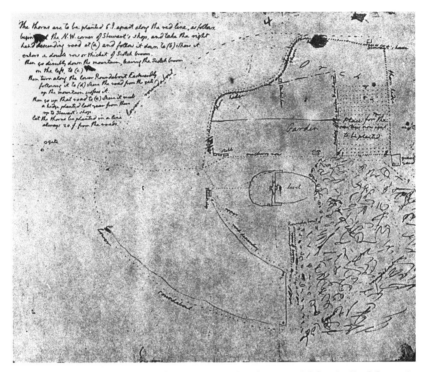

Fig. 44. Monticello, Jefferson's 1806 plan for the top of Monticello Mountain (Massachusetts Historical Society)

drew a spiral.] in the center of it erect a small Gothic temple of antique appearance, appropriate one half to the use of my own family, the other of strangers, servants, etc. erect pedestals with urns, etc., and proper inscriptions. the passage between the walls, 4 f. wide. on the grave of a favorite and faithful servant might be a pyramid erected of the rough rock-stone; the pedestal made plain to receive an inscription. Let the exit of the spiral . . . look on a small and distant part of the blue mountains. in the middle of the temple an alter, the sides of turf, the top of plain stone. very little light, perhaps none at all, save only the feeble ray of a half extinguished lamp.[3]

It was from William Shenstone that Jefferson derived such roman-

---

[3] Betts, *Thomas Jefferson's Garden Book*, p. 25.

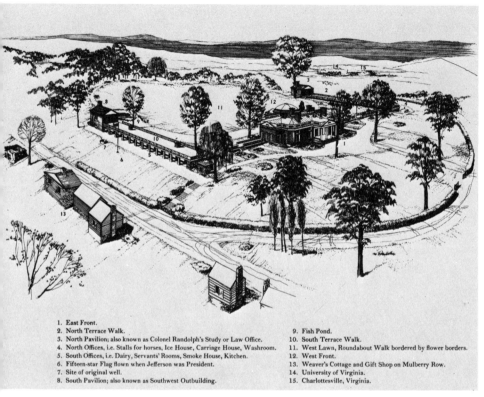

1. East Front.
2. North Terrace Walk.
3. North Pavilion; also known as Colonel Randolph's Study or Law Office.
4. North Offices, i.e. Stalls for horses, Ice House, Carriage House, Washroom.
5. South Offices, i.e. Dairy, Servants' Rooms, Smoke House, Kitchen.
6. Fifteen-star Flag flown when Jefferson was President.
7. Site of original well.
8. South Pavilion; also known as Southwest Outbuilding.
9. Fish Pond.
10. South Terrace Walk.
11. West Lawn, Roundabout Walk bordered by flower borders.
12. West Front.
13. Weaver's Cottage and Gift Shop on Mulberry Row.
14. University of Virginia.
15. Charlottesville, Virginia.

Fig. 45. Monticello, perspective drawing by Frederick Nichols, draftsman Stephen Mathias (Thomas Jefferson Memorial Foundation)

tic ideas as a "Gothic temple of antique appearance." Here Jefferson interrupted his plan with a little poem to his favorite sister, who died in 1765:

Jane Jefferson

'Ah! Joanna, puellarum optima!
Ah! aevi virentis flore praerepta!
Sit tibi terra laevis!
Longe, longeque valeto!'[4]

Spring water was the only kind of water available at Monticello,

---

[4] Shenstone, p. 117; Betts, *Thomas Jefferson's Garden Book*, p. 26.

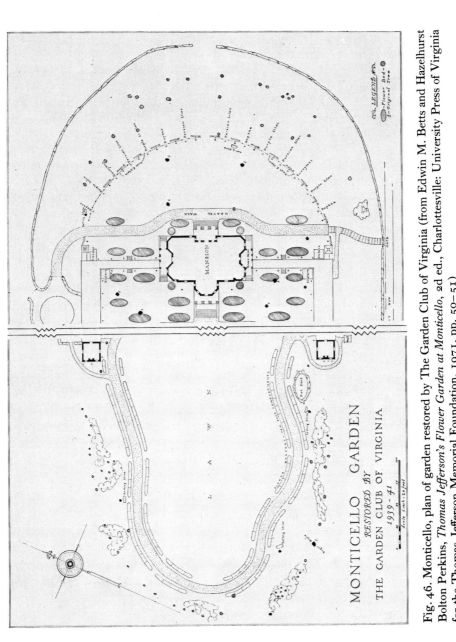

Fig. 46. Monticello, plan of garden restored by The Garden Club of Virginia (from Edwin M. Betts and Hazelhurst Bolton Perkins, *Thomas Jefferson's Flower Garden at Monticello*, 2d ed., Charlottesville: University Press of Virginia for the Thomas Jefferson Memorial Foundation, 1971, pp. 50–51)

but Jefferson intended to utilize it in a very imaginative way:

> at the spring on the North side of the park.
>
> A few feet below the spring level the ground 40 or 50 f. sq. let the water fall from the spring in the upper level over a terrace in the form of a cascade. then conduct it along the foot of the terrace to the Western side of the level, where it may fall into a cistern under a temple, from which it may go off by the western border till it fall over another terrace at the Northern or lower side. let the temple be raised 2. f. for the first floor of stone. under this is the cistern, which may be a bath or anything else. The 1st story arches on three sides, the back or western side being close because the hill there comes down, and also to carry up stairs on the outside. the 2nd story to have a door on one side, a spacious window in each of the other sides, the rooms each 8. f. cube; with a small table and a couple of chairs. the roof may be Chinese,Grecian, or in the taste of the Lantern of Demosthenes at Athens.[5]

The Lantern of Demosthenes is the only Greek building that Jefferson seems to have admired. He also proposed that it form the basis of the design for the Washington Monument. Although Jefferson never got around to building any temples at Monticello, he toyed with such ideas for years. His earliest designs of 1771 for such garden structures were taken directly from James Gibbs's *Book of Architecture*, 1728, plates 67 and 69. Fiske Kimball and later scholars have suggested that his sketches were ideas for garden buildings and that they contained some ideas for the two versions of Monticello, but no one has pointed to their germinal importance. The finished Monticello of 1809 looks almost exactly like Gibbs's plate 67. Thomas Waterman, Clay Lancaster, and others have pointed to Robert Morris's *Select Architecture*, 1755, as Jefferson's source for the second version of the house; however, it is obvious that Morris adopted almost verbatim the design from Gibbs's book, which Jefferson owned by 1770. Jefferson's adaptation of the design for his house was not unlike Scamozzi's design for Rocca Pisana, and both were inspired by Palladio's Villa Rotunda. In fact, Jefferson kept returning to earlier designs during the long course of his architectural practice: in 1817, for the first pavilion of the University of Virginia, he reused one of the first of all the designs for Monticello—a pedimented building with an arcade surmounted by a portico.

Jefferson's 1771 plans continued:

[5] Betts, *Thomas Jefferson's Garden Book*, p. 26.

the ground just about the spring smoothed and turfed; close to the spring a sleeping figure reclined on a plain marble slab, surrounded with turf; on the slab this inscription:

> Hujus nympha loci, sacri custodia fontis
> Dormio, dum blandae sentio murmur aquae
> Parce meum, quisquis tangis cava marmora, sommum
> Rumpere; si bibas, sive lacere, tace.

Near the spring, he specified another Latin inscription praising the rural beauty, to be inscribed "on stone, or a metal plate." Then,

plant trees of Beech and Aspen about it. Open a vista to the millpond, river, road, etc. qu[aere], if a view to the neighboring town would have a good effect? intersperse in this and every other part of the ground (except the environs of the Burying place) abundance of Jesamine, Honeysuckle, sweet briar, etc. under the temple an Aeolian harp, where it may be concealed as well as covered from the weather.

This would be better

the ground above the spring being very steep, dig into the hill and form a cave or grotto. build up the sides and arch with stiff clay. Cover this with moss. spangle it with translucent pebbles from Hanovertown, and beautiful shells from the shore at Burwell's ferry. pave the floor with pebbles. let the spring enter at a corner of the grotto, pretty high up the side, and trickle down, or fall by a spout into a basin, from which it may pass off through the grotto. the figure will be better placed in in this: form a couch of moss. the English inscription will then be proper.

> Nymph of the grot, these sacred springs I keep,
> And to the murmur of these waters sleep;
> Ah! spare my slumbers! gently tread the cave!
> And drink in silence, or in silence lave![6]

All these fanciful ruminations show the delight he took in exploiting every romantic possiblity for his hilltop landscape.

The plans Jefferson wrote in the back of his Account Book in 1771 also included a zoological garden of the type that was a customary part of larger English and Dutch estates.

The ground in General

thin the trees. cut out the stumps and undergrowth. remove old trees and other rubbish, except where they may look well. cover the whole with grass.

[6] Ibid., pp. 26–27.

intersperse Jessamine, honeysuckle, sweetbriar, and even hardy flowers which may not require attention. keep in it deer, rabbits, Peacocks, Guinea poultry, pigeons, etc. let it be an asylum for hares, squirrels, pheasants, partridges, and every other wild animal (except those of prey). court them to it, by laying food for them in proper places. procure a buck-elk, to be, as it were, monarch of the wood; but keep him shy, that his appearance may not lose its effect by too much familiarity. a buffalo might be confined also. inscriptions in various places, on the bark of trees or metal plates, suited to the character or expression of the particular spot.

benches or seats of rock or turf.[7]

Obviously Jefferson was thinking of Shenstone's ideas about a naturalistic garden here, as he was also when he advised John Rutledge, Jr., and Thomas Shippen, while traveling in Europe, to note particularly the gardens of Europe because of the ease with which they may be constructed in the New World, for "the noblest gardens may be made without expense. We have only to cut out the superabundant plants."[8] In Albemarle County honeysuckle grows wild today and, except for its delicious scent in June, would be counted a weed.

West of the house, the owner planned a shrubbery. Alder, barberry, yew, and mountain laurel were to be grown along with vines including the native orange trumpet flower. Other flowers planned were snapdragons, daisies, peonies, and larkspur, along with the ubiquitous periwinkle (*Vinca minor*). Trees included holly, wild cherry, juniper, horse chestnut, and catalpa. This list of plants is the only part of these 1771 plans that Jefferson copied into his Garden Book.

All the details Jefferson so carefully elaborated in 1771 constitute one of the first recorded attempts in America to create a *jardin anglais*. They were all well in accord with the specifications of the authorities in his library.

Two drawings made before or during 1772 show the first version of the house with rectangular flower beds planned for the west front. On the east front what is probably a later addition sketches a semicircle of shrubs and trees (figs. 47, 48). The flower beds may never have been laid out; the shrubs in the east semicircle were put out

[7] Ibid., p. 27.
[8] Lipscomb and Bergh, 17: 281–92.

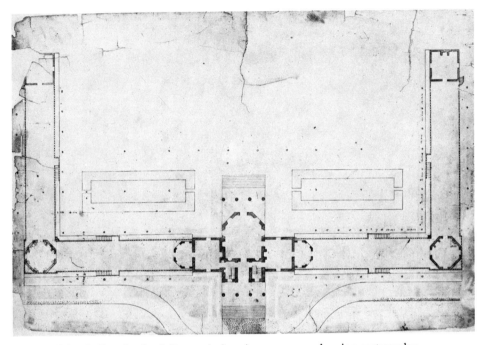

Fig. 47. Monticello, plan by Jefferson, before Aug. 4, 1772, showing rectangular flower beds and proposed temples (never built) at the corners of the terrace walks (Massachusetts Historical Society)

sometime before Jefferson finally ordered his overseer to put in the alternating trees in 1808 or 1809.[9] The more immediate task was not decoration but the growing of vegetables and fruit for food.

Sometime after 1774 Jefferson laid out his first vegetable garden on the slope 44 feet south of Mulberry Row. In the Garden Book, on March 31, 1774, it was stated that the area was 668 feet long and 80 feet wide, with additional triangles at each end (fig. 49). For protection from animals a crude stone wall surrounded the garden.

Mulberry Row was the name of the plantation road to the south of the main house. Along it were located by 1796–1804 some nineteen buildings, including the stable, joinery, stone house, nailery, and an

[9] Edwin M. Betts and Hazelhurst Bolton Perkins, *Thomas Jefferson's Flower Garden at Monticello* (2d ed., Charlottesville, 1971), p. 10.

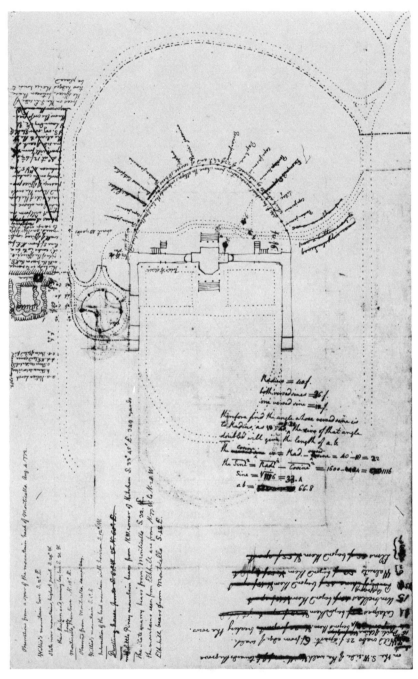

Fig. 48. Monticello, general plan of house and gardens drawn by Jefferson before 1772, with later notations (Massachusetts Historical Society)

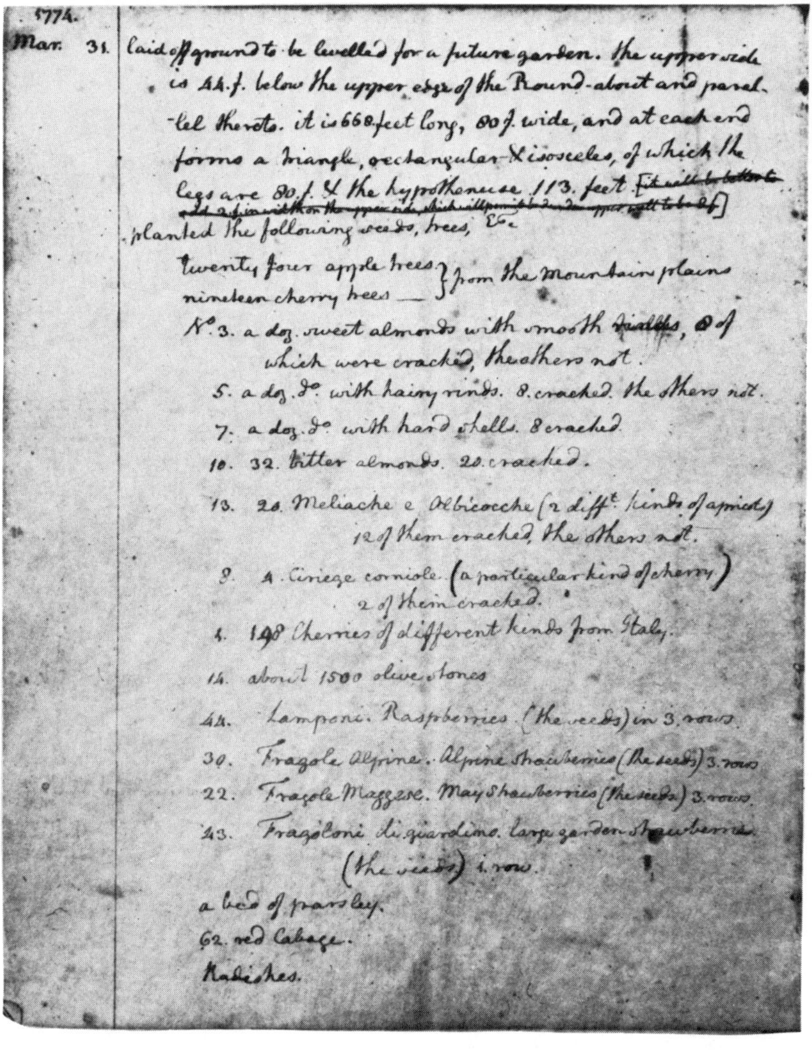

1774.
Mar. 31. laid off ground to be levelled for a future garden. the upper side
is 44.f. below the upper edge of the Round-about and parallel therto. it is 668 feet long, 80 f. wide, and at each end
forms a triangle, rectangular & isosceles, of which the
legs are 80.f. & the hypothenuse 113. feet. [it will be better
to do it in such form that the upper and lower sides may be parallel to each other]
planted the following seeds, trees, &c

Twenty four apple trees ⎫ from the mountain plains
nineteen cherry trees ⎬
                        ⎭

N°.3. a doz. sweet almonds with smooth rinds, 2 of
      which were cracked, the others not.

5. a doz. d°. with hairy rinds. 8. cracked. the others not.

7. a doz. d°. with hard shells. 8 cracked.

10. 32. bitter almonds. 20. cracked.

13. 20. Meliache e Albicocche (2 diff. kinds of apricots)
       12 of them cracked the others not.

9. 4. Cinege corniole (a particular kind of cherry)
      2 of them cracked.

4. 148 Cherries of different kinds from Italy,

14. about 1500 olive stones

44. Lamponi. Raspberries (the seeds) in 3. rows

34. Fragole alpine. Alpine strawberries (the seeds) 3. rows

22. Fragole Maggese. May strawberries (the seeds) 3. rows

43. Fragoloni di giardino. large garden strawberries.
    (the seeds) 4. rows.

a bed of parsley.
62. red Cabage.
Radishes.

Fig. 49. Monticello, page from Jefferson's Garden Book, March 31, 1774 (Massachusetts Historical Society)

unidentified stone structure. There were also log dwellings and utility and necessary houses. It derived its name from the mulberry trees which Jefferson had planted as early as 1771. The Row formed part of the first, or upper, roundabout surrounding the main house. In 1774–78 the first drawing of the buildings was made, and the stone house, or weaver's cottage as it was later known, was begun then.

The siting of the Row forms a barrier between the house and the vegetable and fruit gardens. It is conveniently located, with good orientation, and permits the rest of the grounds to be used for pleasure. It is a well-organized solution to the practical demands of the plantation.

The orchard at Monticello was located on the southeastern slope of the mountain, somewhat west and below the stone house on Mulberry Row. It was first planted in 1769, and included pears, pomgranates, cherries, New York apples, peaches, apricots, almonds, nectarines and figs, which Jefferson particularly liked. In the same general area a plan of an orchard, dated about 1778, was laid out between the second roundabout and the vegetable garden wall. The design shows a grid (fig. 50).

An enthusiastic letter from the orchardist at Monticello, Antonio Giannini, in 1786 describes the orchard:

The apples in the orchard below the garden are producing abundantly. All the varieties of cherry trees are growing well. The "Magnum bonum plumbs" are turning out marvelously and so are the green gages. The apricots are growing satisfactorily. Some died but they have been replaced. The almonds are still alive but are not improving. The peaches are all doing well . . . Has grafted many trees of the kinds TJ requested; but no one had told him about grafting the royal white, yellow, and red peaches. This will be done at once. They have not yet finished planting the apples of the north orchards, but the ones planted are doing well and will have a full crop next autumn.[10]

Before 1793 a north orchard was established on the east side of the house. Over 500 peach trees were planted along the boundaries of selected fields to serve as a tree hedge. Some 870 were planted in the

[10] Julian P. Boyd, ed., *The Papers of Thomas Jefferson* (Princeton, N.J., 1950–), 9:623–24.

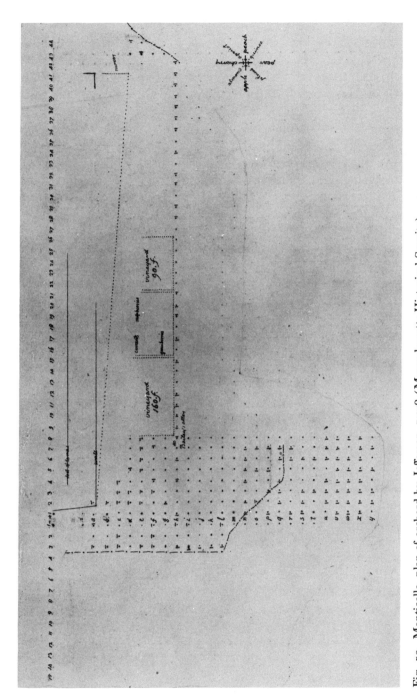

Fig. 50. Monticello, plan of orchard by Jefferson, 1778 (Massachusetts Historical Soceity)

north orchard. In 1811 there were 384 living trees; 84 were apple, 48 cherry, 5 nectarine, 160 peach, 7 apricot, 2 plum, 2 pear, and 5 quince. Plantings were made in 1811 and 1812, but from that time on the orchards began to decline. By 1826, the year of Jefferson's death, some fruit was still being produced by the aged trees.

Probably no other estate in America had the elaborate road system that served Monticello. Before 1769, roads and paths were laid out, and in 1772 the first roundabout was begun. Jefferson not only had to survey the roads but to supervise their building as well. The slaves had to clear them with only conventional tools, but by 1809 there were some twenty miles of roads. Today the roundabouts are the ones that most interest visitors. There were four miles of them, laid like necklaces around the little mountain. The first began at the upper level of the grounds, and they were connected at selected places by oblique paths (fig. 51). Jefferson used these for his daily rides and walks.

Other types of roads included the Northern Path, which gave access to the vital north spring. The Farm Road led into the eastern section of the farm, where the main cultivated fields were located. The Secretary's Ford Road led to Charlottesville across Moore's Creek (fig. 52), while the East, or North, Road went to Shadwell and Orange, and the Three Notched Road to Richmond. The last is thought to have been named because of an Indian trail which was indicated by three cuts in the trees along its length. The South Road, via the Thoroughfare Gap Gate, led to Milton and on to Charlottesville. The Farm Road served the overseer's house, two barns, the halfway house, and the sheep pens, as well as several enclosures known as the Knob, Cooper, Slate Meadow, and North fields (fig. 53), and it was probably the most used road.

Both Shenstone and Lord Kames decried the use of straight entrance drives, so how can it be explained that Jefferson built a straight drive leading to the house at Monticello?[11] In his day the drive led straight across the Rivanna River, and then, still straight, up the mountain through a peach orchard to wooden Chinese trellis gates still in place outside the house. Jefferson was, however, a true architect, who thought in three dimensions. Straight lines in land-

[11] Shenstone, p. 126.

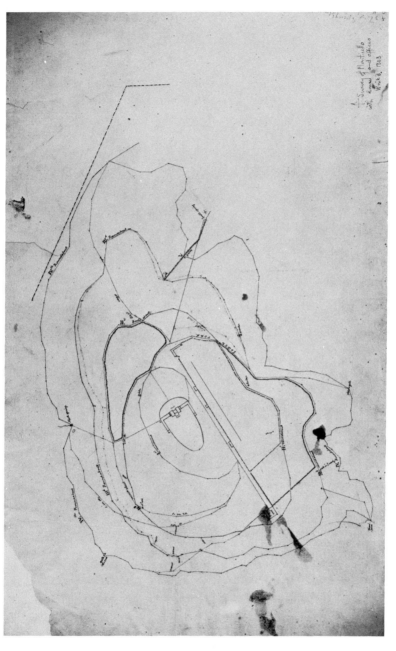

Fig. 51. Monticello, survey of Jefferson showing houses, offices, and four roundabouts, 1803 (Massachusetts Historical Society)

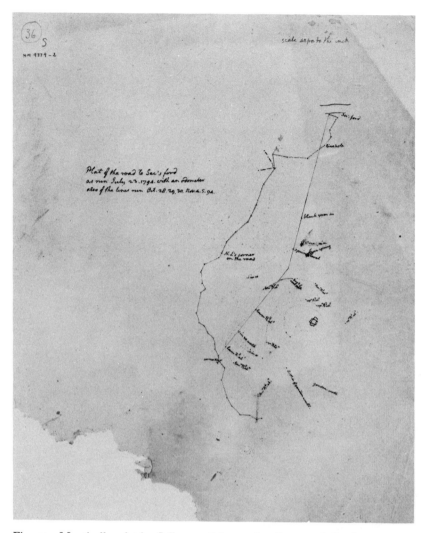

Fig. 52. Monticello, plat by Jefferson of the road to Secretary's Ford, 1794 (The Huntington Library, San Marino, California)

scape bored him and his contemporaries because they provided no element of surprise, as there was when one traveled a curving drive, where the views changed at every turn, leading to a final surprise, the house itself. But since the original drive to Monticello was steep, there was a constantly changing view caused by the undulating

Fig. 53. Monticello, survey of the fields by Jefferson, 1794 (The Huntington Library, San Marino, California)

vertical profile, and the house did not come into view until one had reached the top of the hill, almost at the main gate. As was not unusual, Jefferson compromised his principles, and made a straight drive where the contour of his hilltop did not justify a winding drive. At all of Jefferson's other plantation houses, however, there are curved drives.

During the 1780s and 1790s, two distinguished French visitors were tremendously impressed by Monticello and its setting. The close ties which Jefferson had with nature were described by the marquis de Chastellux in 1782:

There was nothing, in such an unsettled country, to prevent him from fixing his residence wherever he wanted to. But Nature so contrived it, that a Sage and a man of taste should find on his own estate the spot where he might best study and enjoy Her. He called this house *Monticello* (in Italian, Little Mountain), a very modest name indeed, for it is situated upon a very high mountain, but a name which bespeaks the owner's attachments to the language of Italy and above all to the Fine Arts, of which that country was the cradle and is still the resort . . . so that it may be said that Mr. Jefferson is the first American who has consulted the Fine Arts to know how he should shelter himself from the weather. . . . Let me describe to you a man, not yet forty, tall, and with a mild and pleasing countenance, but whose mind and attainments could serve in lieu of all outward graces; an American, who, without ever having quitted his own country, is Musician, Draftsman, Surveyor, Astronomer, Natural Philosopher, Jurist and Statesman.[12]

Perhaps the best description of Monticello and its plantation lands is that of the duc de la Rochefoucauld-Liancourt, who visited it in June 1796:

The house stands on the summit of the mountain, and the taste and arts of Europe have been consulted in the formation of its plan. . . . Monticello, according to its first plan, was infinitely superior to all other houses in America, in point of taste and convenience; but at that time Mr. Jefferson had studied taste and the fine arts in books only. His travels in Europe have supplied him with models; he has appropriated them to his design; and his new plan, the execution of which is already much advanced, will be accomplished before the end of the next year, and then his house will certainly

[12] Chastellux, pp. 390–91.

deserve to be ranked with the most pleasant mansions in France and England.[13]

This French visitor was struck with the care with which Jefferson managed every detail of his farm and buildings, and the good care he took of his workers:

At present he is employed with activity and perseverance in the management of his farms and buildings; and he orders, directs, and pursues in the minutest details every branch of business relative to them. I found him in the midst of the harvest, from which the scorching heat of the sun does not prevent his attendance. His negroes are nourished, clothed, and treated as well as white servants could be. As he can not expect any assistance from the two small neighboring towns, every article is made on his farm: his negroes are cabinetmakers, carpenters, masons, bricklayers, smiths, etc.[14]

Like most plantation owners Jefferson had trouble finding able overseers: either they overworked the slaves and generated rebellions, or they were lazy and shiftless. So, during those periods in which Jefferson was away on public business, the farms generally deteriorated.

Probably in 1804, Jefferson composed an astonishing little essay which confirmed his English-acquired design ideas. He was presumably looking forward to the time when he could retire and supervise the work himself. The first paragraph details changes in Mulberry Row and the vegetable garden.

General ideas for the improvement of Monticello

all the houses on the Mulberry walk to be taken away, except the stone house [the present weaver's house], and a ha! ha! instead of the paling along it for an inclosure. This will of course be made when the garden is levelled, and stone for the wall will be got out of the garden itself, in digging, aided by that got out of the level in front of the S.W. offices, the old stone fence below the stable, and the lower wall of the garden, which is thicker than necessary.[15]

[13] Sarah N. Randolph, *The Domestic Life of Jefferson* (Charlottesville, Va., 1934), pp. 197–98.
[14] Ibid., pp. 244–45.
[15] Kimball, *Thomas Jefferson, Architect*, Figs. 161–62.

A ha-ha is a fence or wall sunk in a grass-covered ditch so as to be invisible from the house, preventing farm animals from getting on the lawn or in the garden. Jefferson had seen ha-ha walls in England, for instance at Stowe, and also in America at Mount Vernon.

In 1802, upon completion of the southeast offices, the slaves had been moved from the log cabins on Mulberry Row to newly completed rooms under the south terrace. The smith's shop, which had been part of the nailery, was moved to a location on the east side of the house. Today the Row consists of the stone house, which is to be restored, and the ruins of the joinery, nailery, the unidentified stone structure, and the stable.

Work was begun in 1809 to create a rectangle, 80 by 1,000 feet, consisting of three terraces. These extended from the barn to the joinery. At the foot of Mulberry Row was the northwest border, where the seedlings were planted. The land was divided into squares of probably 1/27th of an acre, and there were twenty-four in all. Between these were small openings, which joined the northwest border to a grass-covered walk. A stone wall, laid up by the dry method, retained the terrace. The stones were rough native greenstone. It was quite high in places, but most of it has now disappeared. Fortunately, a record was left of how the vegetables were planted, with the same methodical design that characterized all his landscape planting.

A paling fence, ten feet high, was built in 1809 to keep out animals. The palings were not pointed, but had one slanting side, and were to be so close together, as Jefferson directed, "as not to let even a young hare in." [16] They were placed on top of one another on a middle rail in the manner of clapboards, so that one nail would hold them. This arrangement had the advantage of making short pieces of lumber useful.

For his "Garden Olitory," or vegetable garden (fig. 54, 55), he specified: "make the upper slope thus [see fig. 54] at *a* plant a hedgethorn, & at *b* one of privet, or Gleditsia, or cedar to be trimmed down to 3.f. high, the whole appearance thus [see fig. 54]. taking a border of 8.f. at the foot of the terrase for forward productions, the

[16] Betts, *Thomas Jefferson's Garden Book*, p. 317.

Garden. Olitory. make the upper slope thus ⌐ at a plant
a hedge of hedgethorn, & at b one of privet, or Gleditsia, or cedar to
be trimmed down to 3.f. high. the whole appearance thus.
taking a border of 8.f. at the foot of the terras for
forward productions, the main beds must be reduced
from 50.f. to 42.f.

Garden or pleasure grounds.
The canvas at large must be Grove, of the largest trees, (poplar, oak, elm, maple, ash, hiccory, chesnut, Linden, Weymouth pine, sycamore) trimmed very high, so as to give it the appearance of open ground, yet not so far apart but that they may cover the ground with close shade.
this must be broken by clumps of thicket, as the open grounds of the English are broken by clumps of trees.
plants for thickets are broom, calycanthus, althaea, gelder rose, magnolia glauca, azalea, fringe tree, dogwood, redbud, wild crab. kalmia, mezereon, euonymus, halesia, quamoclit, rhododendron, oleander, service tree, lilac, honeysuckle, bramble,
the best way of forming thicket will be to plant it spirally, in labyrinth, putting the tallest plants in the center & lowering gradatim to the external termination. a temple or seat may be in the center.
thus ⟨spiral drawing⟩ leaving space enough between the rows to walk & to trim up, replant &c. the shrubs.
vistas to very interesting objects may be permitted, but in general it is better so to arrange thickets as that they may have the effect of vista in various directions.
Dells or ravines should be a close in trees & undergrowth.
Glens, or hollows should be opened downwards, being embraced by forest.
Glades opened on sloping hill sides, with clumps of trees within them
Temples or seats at those spots on the walks most interesting either for prospect or the immediate scenery
The Broom on the South side to be improved for winter walking or riding, conducting a variety of roads through it, forming chambers with seats, well sheltered from winds, & spread before the sun. a temple with yellow glass panes would suit these, as it would give the illusion of sunshine in cloudy weather.
a thicket may be of cedar, topped into a brush for the center, surrounded by kalmia. or it may be of Scotch broom alone.

Fig. 54. Monticello, Jefferson's plans for "Garden Olitory" and "Garden or pleasure grounds," about 1804 (Massachusetts Historical Society)

Fig. 55. Monticello, vegetable garden as restored by the Thomas Jefferson Memorial Foundation (Frank J. Davis, photographer)

main beds must be reduced from 50.f. to 42.f."[17] This 1804 memo also called for a number of different temples. "At the Rocks" was to be "a turning Tuscan temple 10.f. diam. 6. columns. proportions of Pantheon," and "at the Point," he proposed to "build Demosthenes's lantern"; at the two elbows of the terrace walks, over the offices, were

[17] Kimball, *Thomas Jefferson Architect*, Figs. 161–62. "Garden Olitory": Latin "Olitorius or better Holitorius meaning of or belonging to a kitchen garden or to vegetables" (Charlton T. Lewis and Charles Short, *A Latin Dictionary* [1879: rept. Oxford, 1955]).

to be erected copies of "the Chinese pavilion of Kew garden." Then "along the lower edge of the garden" he proposed to place four small temples, models of the Gothic style; the Pantheon, which he regarded the masterpiece of spherical building; a "model of cubic architecture," such as the Maison Carrée; and "a specimen of Chinese" architecture. These were all to be connected by an arbor. After making these notes, he changed his mind about the location, saying: "The kitchen garden is not the place for ornaments of this kind. bowers and treillages suit that better, & these temples will be better disposed in the pleasure grounds."[18] Bricks for the temples were ordered in December 1807, but they were never built. Nor were the Chinese pavilions.

The "Garden or pleasure grounds" were to be laid out as carefully as a painter would compose a landscape. How well Jefferson knew his native plants:

The canvas at large must be Grove, of the largest trees, (poplar, oak, elm, maple, ash, hickory, chestnut, Linden, Weymouth pine, sycamore) trimmed very high, so as to give it the appearance of open ground, yet not so far apart but that they may cover the ground with close shade.

This must be broken by clumps of thicket, as the open grounds of the English are broken by clumps of trees. plants for thickets are broom, calycanthus, altheas, gelder rose, magnolia glauca, azalea, fringe tree, dogwood, red bud, wild crab, kalmia, mezereon, euonymous, halesia, quamoclid, rhododendron, oleander, service tree, lilac, honeysuckle, brambles.[19]

This admirer of water in the landscape regretted the lack of a large body of water at Monticello, but he always planned to use the spring for decorative purposes, specifying in the 1804 plan: "The spring of Montalto [Carter's Mountain] either to be brought to Monticello by pipes or to fall over steps of stairs in cascade, made visible at Monticello through a vista."[20] Furthermore, he used a reflecting pool, which also served to keep fish fresh for the table.

Jefferson learned well the use of vistas in landscape. His 1804 essay goes on: "The ground between the upper & lower roundabouts to be laid out in lawns & clumps of trees, the lawns opening so as to give advantageous catches of prospect to the upper roundabout.

[18] Kimball, *Thomas Jefferson, Architect*, Figs. 161–62.
[19] Ibid.
[20] Ibid.

Vistas from the lower roundabout to good portions of prospect walks in this style [diagram of walks crossing roundabouts at angles], winding up the mountain."[21]

Jefferson did not neglect to design his terraces and slopes:

Vistas to very interesting objects may be permitted, but in general it is better so to arrange the thickets as that they may have the effect of vista in various directions.

Dells and ravines should be close in trees & undergrowth.

Glens, or hollows should be opened downwards, being embraced by forest.

Glades opened on sloping hill sides, with clumps of trees within them

Temples or seats at those spots on the walks most interesting either for prospect or the immediate scenery.

The Broom wilderness on the South side to be improved for winter walking or riding, conducting a variety of roads through it, forming chambers with seats, well sheltered from winds, & spread before the sun. a temple with yellow glass panes would suit these, as it would give the illusion of sunshine in cloudy weather.

a thicket may be of Cedar, topped into a bush, for the center, surrounded by Kalmia. or it may be of Scotch broom alone.[22]

These ideas, clearly influenced by English landscape gardening, were set on paper about 1804, as the date September 4, 1804, appears in the notes. In these notes, Jefferson was thinking out loud about ideas he expressed in his later letter to William Hamilton in 1806.

Early in 1806, Jefferson began a new planting plan which shows his revived interest in the English landscape style. In February he sent it to be planted by John Freeman, who was then an overseer. It shows the present terraced kitchen garden between the overseer Bailey's house and Mulberry Row and the graveyard at the northwest corner of the orchard. Instructions were given for planting trees in the southwest orchard and thorn hedges along the second roundabout on the northeast side. A double row of Scotch broom was also to be planted near the first and second roundabouts. In May the North Road was completed.[23]

On June 7, 1807, in a letter to his granddaughter Anne Cary

---

[21] Kimball, *Thomas Jefferson, Architect*, Figs. 161–62.

[22] Ibid.

[23] Betts, *Thomas Jefferson's Garden Book*, pp. 310, 312, 316.

Randolph, who adored gardening, he sketched his plan for flower beds near the house and the winding walk and flower borders for the west lawn (fig. 56). He had just completed the plantings immediately around the house. The trees included purple beeches, paper mulberries, mountain ashes, one redbud, horse chestnuts, and balsam poplars. In the "Clumps" on the east side of the house he had planted pinks, carnations, Ixia chinensis, Jeffersonia, SweetWilliam, yellow horned poppy, "Everlasting pea," and "Flowering pea." On the west front he put amaryllis, anemone, tulips, Columbian lillies, poppies, winter cherries, lobelia, lychnis, ranunculus, tuberoses, lavatera, and hyacinths.[24]

The following year the serpentine walk on the west lawn and the beds bordering it were laid out (fig. 57). In 1812 he decided to reorder these flower borders, planting each kind of flower in its own "compartment" rather than mixing varieties.

flower borders. Apr, 8. laid them off into compartments of 10.f. length each.
in the N. borders are 43. ⎫ compartments.
in the S. borders are 44½ ⎭
the odd compartments are for bulbs required taking up
the even ones for seeds & permanent bulbs.
denote the inner borders .1. and the outer .o.
Apr. 8. sowed Bellflower in 28. on both sides
African Marigold 32d. do.
White poppy 42d. N. and 44th. S.[25]

One of Jefferson's granddaughters has left a delightful picture of Jefferson in his old age. It shows the great pleasure he took in his grandchildren as well as in his garden:

He loved farming and gardening, the fields, the orchards, and his asparagus-beds. Every day he rode through his plantation and walked in his garden. In the cultivation of the last he took great pleasure. Of flowers, too, he was very fond. One of my early recollections is of the attention which he paid to his flower beds. He kept up a correspondence with persons in the large cities, particularly, I think, in Philadelphia, for the purpose of receiving supplies of roots and seeds both for his kitchen and flower garden. I remember well, when he first returned to Monticello [after his retirement]

[24] Ibid., pp. 333–335, Plate XXIII.
[25] Ibid., pp. 474, 477, Plates XXIV, XXXIV.

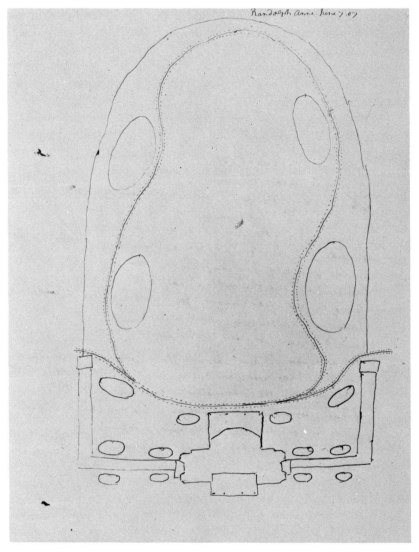

Fig. 56. Monticello, plan of serpentine walk and oval flower beds by Jefferson about 1807 (Histocial Society of Pennsylvania)

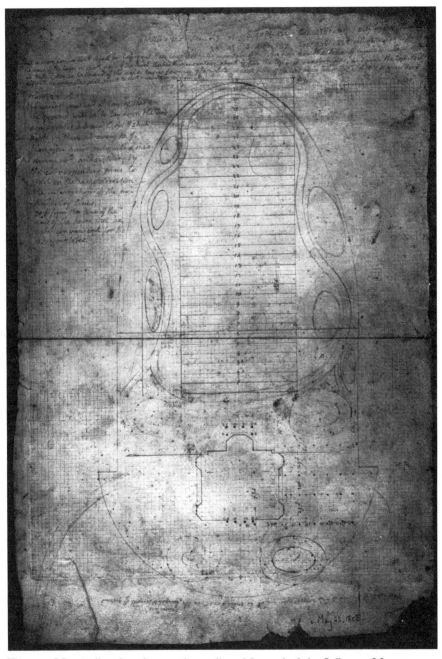

Fig. 57. Monticello, plan of serpentine walk and flower beds by Jefferson, May 23, 1808 (Massachusetts Historical Soceity)

how immediately he began to prepare new beds for his flowers. He had these beds laid off on the lawn, under the windows, and many a time I have run after him when he went out to direct the work, accompanied by one of his gardeners, generally Wormley, armed with spade and hoe, while he himself carried the measuring line.

I was too young to aid him, except in a small way but my sister, Mrs. Bankhead, then a young and beautiful woman, was his active and useful assistant. I remember the planting of the first hyacinths and tulips, and their subsequent growth. The roots arrived labelled, each with a fancy name. There was "Marcus Aurelius" and the "King of the Gold Mine," the "Roman Empress" and the "Queen of the Amazons," "Psyche," the "God of Love," etc., etc. Eagerly, and with childish delight, I studied this brilliant nomenclature, and wondered what strange and surprisingly beautiful creations I should see arising from the ground when spring returned; and, these precious roots were committed to the earth under my grandfather's own eye, with his beautiful granddaughter Anne standing by his side, and a crowd of happy young faces, of younger grandchildren, clustering round to see the progress, and inquire anxiously the name of each separate deposit.

Then, when spring returned, how eagerly we watched the first appearance of the shoots above ground. Each root was marked with its own name written on a bit of stick by its side; and what joy it was for one of us to discover the tender green breaking through the mould, and run to grandpapa to announce that we really believed Marcus Aurelius was coming up, or the Queen of the Amazons was above ground! With how much pleasure, compounded of our pleasure and his own, on the new birth, he would immediately go out to verify the fact, and praise us for our diligent watchfulness.

Then, when the flowers were in bloom, and we were in ecstasies over the rich purple and crimson, or pure white, or delicate lilac or pale yellow of the blossoms, how he would sympathize with our admiration, or discuss with my mother and elder sister new groupings and combinations and contrasts. Oh, these were happy moments for us and for him![26]

After 1812, he almost ceased to record flowers in his Garden Book. Other interests seem to have occupied his time, but, more important, he probably had all the decorative plants he wanted, and his entries are chiefly concerned with his vegetable gardens. In 1831 James Barclay, the second owner of Monticello, attempted to estab-

[26] Henry S. Randall, *Life of Thomas Jefferson* (139th ed., Richmond, 1858), 3: 346–47.

lish silkworms; to plant mulberry trees for them he plowed under the flower gardens and destroyed many of Jefferson's favorite trees. Fortunately, in recent years the flower beds have been carefully restored by The Garden Club of Virginia according to Jefferson's plans under the direction of Hazelhurst Bolton Perkins and the late Edwin M. Betts, professor of biology at the University of Virginia (figs. 58–60).[27]

Working carefully with native materials, although he was constantly experimenting with exotic plants, and with the topography at hand, Jefferson created at Monticello a very original version of a landscape garden. If his ideas were only partially realized, it was because the contours and his finances did not permit the complete realization of the garden in his mind. It is that imaginary garden he created on paper that we admire, as splendid as any of those of the period of romantic classicism that he had studied so carefully in England.

Jefferson never lived in any house without trying to change it, and it seems the gardens he leased were no exception. In Paris at the beautiful Hôtel de Langeac, where he lived most of the time he was in France, he redesigned the garden. It is not sure how much of it he actually changed, but his several drawings show an ingeniously laid out *jardin anglais*, or informal plan, with winding paths and a little mound to view the whole (fig. 61).

When he returned to Virginia, and his friends requested advice on their buildings and gardens, he advised James Madison at Montpelier in Orange County, and was undoubtedly responsible for its delightful icehouse. It is an ideal garden temple with a dome surmounting a circular icehouse (fig. 62). This circular domed temple in the Doric order combines beauty with utility in a typical Jeffersonian manner.[28]

Many other friends sought Jefferson's help in building, but there is little evidence of his influence on their site planning. Belle Grove in Frederick County and Bremo in Fluvanna County are distinguished Virginia plantations whose designs are partially attributed to Jeffer-

[27] See Betts and Perkins.
[28] A drawing of such a monopteros survives, made by Jefferson after 1804; see Frederick Doveton Nichols, *Thomas Jefferson's Architectural Drawings* (1961; rev. and en. 3d ed., Boston and Charlottesville, 1971), p. 38 (no. 183).

Fig. 58. Monticello, serpentine walk as restored by The Garden Club of Virginia (Frank J. Davis, photographer)

son. Bremo is sited on the crest of a hill after Jefferson's favorite arrangement, but his chief housewright, John Neilson, is named as the architect in the cornerstone. But these two houses did not contribute as much to his reputation as a site planner as the plantations he is authentically known to have designed for himself and friends.

Edgemont, located in Albemarle County overlooking the Hardware River valley, is a typical example of Jefferson's imaginative skill in planning a house to fit harmoniously into a natural hillside.

Fig. 59. Monticello, oval flower beds restored as laid out by Jefferson (Frank J. Davis, photographer)

Designed for his friend James Powell Cocke in 1793,[29] this two-level house still stands as a testimonial to Jefferson's genius as a site planner. Although the gardens have been altered, the basic anatomy of the landscape setting remains intact. On the upper side the house at the main entrance is only one story high. But from the approach by the road below the first glimpse is of a two-story house. From this

[29] Jefferson Papers, Library of Congress.

Fig. 60. Monticello, bird's-eye view of serpentine walk as restored by The Garden Club of Virginia (Christopher Bene, photographer)

point where the house is first seen the drive winds up the slope until it enters the courtyard on the upper level where a full view of the house is revealed. This scheme, not unpremeditated by Jefferson, produces a pleasant surprise. On the lower level an arcade opens on ground level to a garden that appears to be on natural grade (fig. 63). From there the slope descends by "falling terraces" down the river valley.

Barboursville, like other Jefferson-designed houses, has a beautiful site, but not a typical Jefferson site poised on the crest of a slope. It is located between two low hills with beautiful views of distant mountains. But it is unusual for Jefferson in that it is on a flat site (fig. 64). It is apparent that he helped to plan the location as well as the

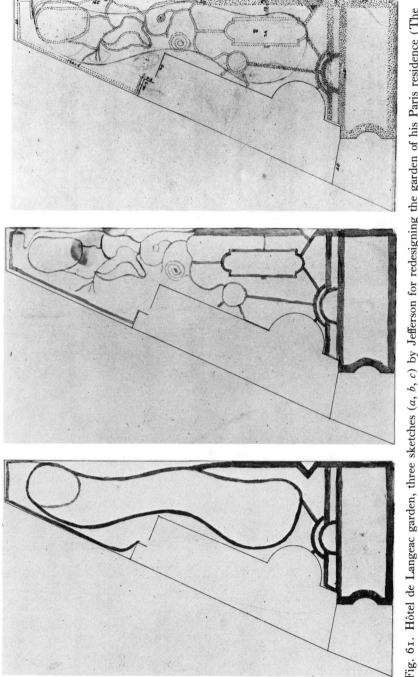

Fig. 61. Hôtel de Langeac garden, three sketches (*a*, *b*, *c*) by Jefferson for redesigning the garden of his Paris residence (The Huntington Library, San Marino, California)

Fig. 62. Montpelier, Virginia, home of James Madison, combination icehouse and garden pavilion designed by Jefferson (Ralph E. Griswold, photographer)

Fig. 63. Edgemont, Albemarle County, designed by Jefferson for James Powell Cocke, 1793

house because his 1817 drawing, with specifications on the back, is for a horizontal area.[30] However, the house is oriented so that the portico shades the octagonal drawing room during the hottest part of the day, which was a firm Jefferson design concept.

Edgehill is also in Albemarle County, not far from Monticello. The house was begun in 1798 by Thomas Mann Randolph, who married Jefferson's daughter Martha. Drawings of the house by Jefferson exist. Its site is set against the Southwest Mountains in typical Jeffersonian style with panoramas of rolling farmlands. The original entrance lined with Virginia cedar trees resembled the allées of cypress trees Jefferson had seen in Italy. Jefferson carried on a prolific correspondence with his daughter Martha and his grand-daughter Ellen about plants and gardens which indicate his lively interest in the landscape at Edgehill. Later the first house was moved back and the site was used for the present house, rebuilt after a fire about 1840.

Poplar Forest, Bedford County, was, next to Monticello, Jeffer-

---

[30] Item k206, Massachusetts Historical Society.

Fig. 64. Ruins of Barboursville, Orange County, designed by Jefferson for James Barbour, 1817 (Mario di Valmarana; David Watson, photographer)

son's finest achievement in site planning (fig. 65). He was very fond of this quiet plantation and had written his *Notes on the State of Virginia* there. He began construction of an unusual octagonal house in 1806 to serve as a retreat from the continual stream of visitors at Monticello. The unusual shape of the house was carried into the garden where octagonal terraces carry out the same theme in the landscape. Even the pair of "necessary houses," or privies, which are separated from the house by artificial mounds and trees, repeat the octagonal form. Building on a slope, Jefferson took advantage of the natural terrain to have both the upper and lower floors open directly onto ground levels. By this scheme he merged the interior floor levels with the exterior grades, creating an intimacy with the landscape that was unique with him in this country. Jefferson constantly referred to Popular Forest as his retreat where he tried to rest and concentrate on his many problems. It was, therefore, not a place for elaborate gardens demanding attention. On the contrary, it represents the opposite end of the gamut of landscape planning from Monticello. Jefferson was a versatile planner capable of fitting his design to its use.

Fig. 65. Poplar Forest, Bedford County, Virginia, designed and built by Jefferson, begun in 1806 (drawn by Frederick Spitzmiller)

CHAPTER VI

Horticultural Influence

Next to architecture, Jefferson's second love was horticulture. He surpassed all his contemporaries for the breadth and precision of his knowledge in this field. Yet he did not use his horticultural knowledge for purely scientific purposes. As usual, he applied it to practical problems of agriculture, gardening, and "embellishment of grounds by fancy." With his insatiable curiosity about everything that grows he lost no opportunity to increase his knowledge of plants for utility and ornament. While he was no Linnaeus he respected and made use of the Linnaean system of plant identification.[1] The plants he discovered and introduced can, therefore, be identified scientifically with the ones commonly used by landscape architects.

Jefferson practiced a kind of humanized horticulture that enhanced his personal friendships. In fact, his letters to friends exchanging plant favors are the best source of information about his phenomenal interest in the dissemination of knowledge about plant discovery, propagation, and usefulness. Fortunately, these letters are included in Edwin Bett's edition of the Garden Book. This book and his Farm Book, also edited by Betts, are a record of his horticultural interest as good as his *Notes on the State of Virginia* is for his interest in natural history. The magnitude of this special interest is indicated by the 662 pages of the printed *Garden Book*. Amazing as this magnitude is, it is not as impressive as the quality of detail, evident from the day he first began his horticultural diary, after his return home to Shadwell from college (fig. 66). His last entry for that day, May 11, 1766, says: "the purple flag, Dwarf flag, Violet & wild Honeysuckle still in bloom. went journey to Maryland, Pennsyl-

---

[1] Carlos Linnaeus (1707–1778), Swedish scientist, was the author of *Systema Naturae, Philosophia Botanica*, and *Species Plantarum*; all three and several others were in Jefferson's library. In a letter from Monticello in 1814 to Dr. John Manners, in defense of Linnaeus's plant classification, Jefferson pointed out that the most important consideration was that Linnaeus's method unites "all nations under one language in Natural History" (Betts, *Thomas Jefferson's Garden Book*, pp. 528–31).

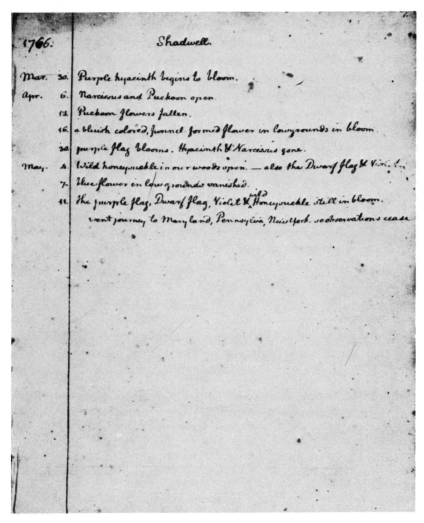

Fig. 66. Page 1 of Jefferson's Garden Book (Massachusetts Historical Society)

vania, New York, so observations cease."[2] Later on there were other
interruptions in his Garden Book recordings while he was in France
and while he was in the nation's service in Philadelphia and Washing-

[2] Ibid, p. 1.

ton, but the continuity was maintained by his correspondence.

It is impossible to do justice to Jefferson's horticultural influence without referring frequently to his friendly collaborator, Bernard McMahon. He was author of *The American Gardener's Calendar*, a practical seed grower, and a plant propagator whose greenhouses were outside Philadelphia.[3] When Jefferson distributed the plant materials from Lewis and Clark's journey across the continent in 1804.–6 to the propagators he considered most reliable, he chose McMahon as one of them. Later he sent portions to Dr. David Hosack, director of the New York Botanical Garden, and to William Hamilton in Philadelphia. To McMahon he wrote in 1813, "if you could make up a collection of the seeds of the plants brought to us by Governor Lewis from beyond the Missisipi, it would be a just and grateful return which M. Thoüin merits at our hands. he expresses to me a great desire for the plants of the region beyond the Mississipi."[4] The shipments of seeds, of which there were many received from M. André Thoüin, the director of the Jardins des Plantes in Paris, were also consigned to McMahon for his tender care. For his planting at Monticello, Jefferson bought from McMahon seeds, bulbs, shrubs, and trees almost every year. Their correspondence could, in itself, make a book on nineteenth-century landscape planting.

A great many trees which this great horticultural experimenter was instrumental in introducing for ornamental planting are commonly grown in the eastern United States. Among his colleagues in

[3] Bernard McMahon, *The American Gardener's Calendar* (11th ed., with introd. by William Darlington, Philadelphia, 1857), p. xi: "Bernard M'Mahon was no common man. He sought the American shores from political motives. . . . The writer well remembers his store, his garden, and greenhouses. The latter situated near the Germantown turnpike, between Philadelphia and Nicetown. . . . I renewed the acquaintance in 1802, 3, and 4 . . . by which time he had established his nurseries of useful and ornamental plants. . . . He was a regularly educated gardener, of much experience and great enterprise. He gave the first decisive impulse to scientific horticulture in our state; and to him we are mainly indebted . . . for the successful culture and dissemination of the interesting novelties collected by Lewis and Clarke, in their journey to the Pacific."

[4] Betts, *Thomas Jefferson's Garden Book*, p. 513. One of the plants collected by Lewis and Clark was snowberry, *Symphoracarpos racemosa*, described by Jefferson as "beautiful in autumn and winter by it's bunches of snow white berries" (ibid., p. 568). This plant is now commonly used for shady locations, winter bird food, and ornament throughout northern America.

this enterprise was William Hamilton, who wrote from his home, The Woodlands, on July 7, 1806:

N.B. In the autumn I intend sending you if I live three kinds of trees which I think you will deem valuable additions to your garden viz—*Gingko biloba* or China Maidenhair tree, *Broussenetia papyrifera* vulgarly called paper mulberry tree & *Mimosa julibrisin* or silk tree of Constantinople. The first is said by Kossmyler [?] to produce a good eatable nut—the 2nd in the bark as yields a valuable material for making paper to the inhabitants of China, Japan, & the East Indies, & for clothing to the people of Otaheite [probably Tahiti] & other South Sea Islands—& the third is a beautiful flowering tree at this time in its highest perfection, the seeds of which were collected on the shore of the Caspian Sea. They are all hardy having for several years past borne our severest weather in the open ground without the smallest protection.[5]

Hamilton's statement that the gingko bears "a good eatable nut" shows his lack of experience with the foul-smelling fruit of the mature female tree. Very few people could withstand the odor long enough to extract the seed for eating. It may be assumed from this reference that *Gingko biloba* was not known in this country (except in fossilized geological form) before Hamilton's introduction of it ca. 1806, which eliminates it for authentic restoration planting of eighteenth-century landscapes. Its subsequent widespread use as a city street tree and, in its fastigiate form, for emphatic accents puts all landscape designers in debt to these two gentleman plant importers (fig. 67).

As for the other two plants mentioned by Hamilton, the first, the paper mulberry tree, will be recognized as the grotesquely knarled trunks that are picturesque features in the Colonial Williamsburg landscape (fig. 68). The second, the mimosa, spreads its feathery pink plumage over Virginia and Carolina countrysides every summer (fig. 69).

The Woodlands, considered by Jefferson as "the only rival which I have known in America to what may be seen in England,"[6] was referred to later by the landscape gardener Andrew Jackson Downing as the finest example of an English naturalistic landscape in America (fig. 70). Jefferson's ultimate regard for The Woodlands

[5] Ibid., pp. 320–21.
[6] Ibid., p. 323.

Fig. 67. *Ginkgo biloba*, maidenhair tree, near Rotunda, University of Virginia
(Frank J. Davis, photographer)

Fig. 68. *Broussenetia papyrifera*, paper mulberry (Ralph E. Griswold, photographer)

was shown in his 1807 letter to Dr. Casper Wistar, for whom the beautiful vine wistaria was named: "I have a grandson, the son of Mr. Randolph, now about fifteen years of age, in whose education I take a lively interest. . . . I am not a friend to placing young men in populous cities, because they acquire there habits and partialities which do not contribute to the happiness of their after life. But there are particular branches of science, which are not so advantageously taught anywhere else in the United States as in Philadelphia. The garden at the Woodlands for Botany, Mr. Peale's Museum for Natural History, your Medical school for Anatomy, and the able professors in all of them, give advantages not to be found elsewhere. We propose, therefore, to send him to Philadelphia to attend the schools of Botany, Natural History, Anatomy."[7]

Unfortunately, the grounds of The Woodlands, having been con-

[7] Ibid., p. 349.

Fig. 69. *Albizzia julibrisson*, silk tree, also called mimosa in southern United States (Frank J. Davis, photographer)

verted to a modern cemetery, bear no relation to the original land-scape. Some few very old gingko trees that remain standing may have been planted by Hamilton. There is, however, ample evidence that Hamilton shared Jefferson's taste for classical architecture. To the mansion that he inherited he added a Doric portico standing high above the ground overlooking the Schuylkill valley. In 1788 after a trip to England he altered and enlarged the house and built the handsome stable and coach house as they are still preserved. There was also "a greenhouse whose front, including the hothouses on each side, measured one hundred and forty feet." It was undoubtedly in this greenhouse that the plant was grown that Jefferson referred to when he wrote Hamilton, on April 22, 1800: "Among the many botanical curiosities you were so good as to shew me the other day, I forgot to ask if you had the *Dionaea muscipula* [Venus's flytrap], & whether it produces a seed with you. If it does, I should be very much disposed to trespass on your liberality so far as to ask a few seeds of that, as also of the *Acacia Nilotica*, or *Farnesiana*, whichever you

Fig. 70. The Woodlands, estate of William Hamilton, Philadelphia, drawn by William Strickland (collection of Ralph Griswold)

have."[8] Here the master diplomat showed his deference to the jealous guardianship felt by almost all plant collectors for their prize items.

As a prelude to his most important landscape undertakings at Monticello, Jefferson had what amounted to a self-directed five-year postgraduate course of European travel. Incidental to a diplomatic mission to France for the United States government he made valuable horticultural friendships which led to a lifetime of international plant exchanges. With Paris as his base he explored all of France (fig. 71), parts of Italy, and much of Germany, Belgium, and Holland. He studied agricultural products in northern Italy and visited English gardens with Whately's *Observations on Modern Gardening* in hand. This experience made him the best-informed American observer, if not the most knowledgeable designer of architecture and gardening,

[8] Ibid., p. 271.

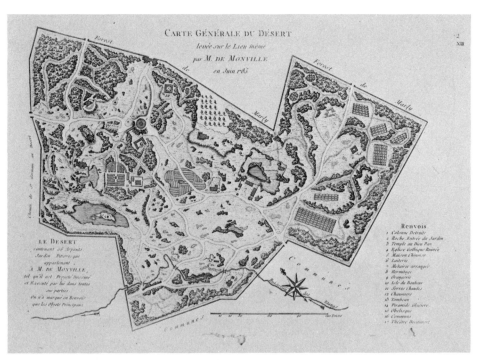

Fig. 71. Plan of the garden of Le Désert de Retz visited by Jefferson (from George Louis LeRouge, *Des Jardins Anglo-Chinois*, Paris, 1776–88, cahier XIII, pl. 2, The Dumbarton Oaks Garden Library)

both amateur and professional, in the newly created United States of America.

In Paris, M. Thoüin of the Jardins des Plantes became a highly respected friend and collaborator in plant exchanges. Jefferson wrote in 1808 to his daughter, Martha Jefferson Randolph: "tell Anne that my old friend Thouin . . . has sent me 700 species of seed. I suppose they will contain all the fine flowers of France, and fill all the space we have for them [at Monticello]." Later he sent these seeds to McMahon for propagation, fearing that they might not receive proper attention at Monticello. Again, in 1811 he wrote McMahon: "My old friend Thouin . . . has just sent me a fresh parcel of seeds which he thus describes. 'They consist of about 200. species, foreign to N. America, selected from among 1. the large trees, the wood of which is useful in the arts. 2. small trees & shrubs, ornamental for shrubberies. 3. plants vivacious & picturesque. 4. flowers for parterres. 5. plants for use in medicine & all the branches of rural & domestic economy.'"[9] Only by a man of vivid imagination like Thoüin could plants be described as "vivacious & picturesque."

Jefferson also carried on a lively exchange of native American seeds and plants with an aunt of the marquis de Lafayette, the comtesse de Noailles de Tessé (fig. 72), with whom he enjoyed a stimulating horticultural correspondence that he sadly missed when he returned to Washington where he lamented: "my present situation is not favorable. . . . not a single person in this quarter has attended to botanical subjects beyond the ordinary produce of the kitchen garden." He arranged to have shipments of Virginia plants sent to her in 1788–90 through his friends John Bartram, Jr., and McMahon. But during the second term of his presidency, he wrote her, "On the 26th of October 1805 I had the pleasure of writing to you, and of informing you that I then made up for you a box of seeds acorns and nuts, which were to go by a vessel bound from Baltimore to Nantes . . . which I fear proved finally abortive." Persistence prompted another attempt, and, he continued, "I had made up another box for you. . . . it is divided into 15 cells, numbered from I to XV & containing as follows Cell No. I Quercus Phellos II 2 Palestris or Rubra dissecta III 2 Prinos IV 2 Alba V VI IX Liriodendron tulipifera VII VIII Juniperus Virginiana X XI Bignonia Catalpa XII Cornus Florida XIII Juglans nigra, & in a bag some Lima beans for your garden. I never saw them in France. XIV Juglans Paccan & in a bag some Arachis hypogasa [peanuts] XV Diospyros Virginiana [persimmon]." Thus anyone who eats lima beans in France probably has Jefferson to thank. The care he took with his shipment shows the feeling he had for this friendship. In return Jefferson received from the comtesse "seeds of Paullinia or Koelreuteria, "one of which," he informed her, "has germinated, and is now growing."[10] Edwin Betts says, "So far as I have been able to ascertain, Jefferson was the first one to plant this tree in Albemarle County."[11] This highly ornamental, late-spring-flowering golden-

[9] Ibid., pp. 378, 456.
[10] Ibid., pp. 284, 188, 339, 454.
[11] Ibid., p. 398.

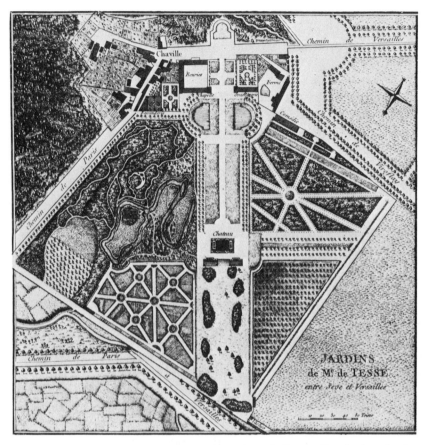

Fig. 72. Chaville, estate of Madame de Tessé (from LeRouge, *Des Jardins Anglo-Chinois*, cahier III, pl. 23, courtesy of Julian P. Boyd, *The Papers of Thomas Jefferson*, Princeton University Press)

rain tree has since become one of the most popular trees for landscape planting (fig. 73).

This correspondence between two ardent plant lovers was, it should be noted, a strictly scientific name relationship; no vulgar or common names were used. To the comtesse he repeatedly sent boxes of plants that, on account of the French Revolution and piracy of the high seas, never reached their destination. Yet he used every device at his disposal; while president of the United States he asked the captain of a ship carrying "gun carriages to the Emperor of Morocco"

Fig. 73. *Koelreuteria paniculata*, goldenrain tree (Frank J. Davis, photographer)

and "the ratification of our late treaty with France" to take her "a box of plants" weighing "about three quarters of a ton."[12] His directions

[12] Ibid., p. 289.

for delivering the treaty were no more explicit than those for delivering the plants. A 1,500-pound box of plants was not exactly a trivial tribute nor was it intended as such. As a postscript to his long letter of October 26, 1805, he added: "since writing the above I have been able to get some of the Pyrus coronaria, or malus sylvestris virginiana floribus odoratis of Clayton. both the blossom and apple are of the finest perfume, and the apple is the best of all possible burnishers for brass and steel furniture which has contracted rust."[13] Such an appreciation of Virginia's wild sweet crabapple, used prolifically by landscape architects for naturalistic planting, is a tribute to Jefferson's aesthetic and practical horticultural sense.

An earlier English botanist, John Banister, Sr., preceded Jefferson's *Notes on the State of Virginia* with his seventeenth-century notes on natural history. According to John Lawson in 1709, "Had not the ingenius Mr. Banister the greatest Virtuoso we ever had on this continent been unfortunately taken out of this world" by a fatal accident in the field "he would have given the best Account of the Plants of America."[14] His grandson, John Banister, Jr., was helpful to Jefferson by facilitating shipment of plants to the comtesse de Noailles de Tessé. Curiously, in all his French horticultural correspondence Jefferson wrote hardly a word about design, perhaps because he did not admire French gardens. During his short visit to England the reverse happened; his comments primarily concerned design.

When Jefferson arrived in Paris, John Adams and Benjamin Franklin were still there, but Franklin soon went back to the United States and Adams was transferred to London. Adams was still at the Court of St. James's when Jefferson was sent over from France for a special diplomatic errand. But he was not too busy to induce Adams to join him on a tour of English gardens. This tour had long been in Jefferson's mind; he had already prepared himself by reading Whately's *Observations on Modern Gardening*, which he carried with him as a constant guide. His comments in his memorandum of the March and April 1786 trip, as we have seen, revealed his own taste in architecture and gardening. His general opinion of England was

[13] Ibid., p. 306.

[14] Joseph Ewan and Nesta Ewan, *John Banister and His Natural History of Virginia, 1678–1692* (Urbana, Ill, 1970), p. 141.

expressed later in a letter to his friend John Page of Virginia: "The gardening in that country is the article in which it surpasses all the earth. I mean their pleasure gardening. This, indeed, went far beyond my ideas." No such appraisal of the French formal gardens had been offered. Indirectly, though, his opinion of the florid, formal French LeNôtre style was expressed about the German gardens at Schwetzingen (fig. 74), an exaggerated example of this grandiose kind of garden that "show[s] how much money may be laid out to make an ugly thing, what is called the English quarter, however relieves the eye from the straight rows of trees, round and square basins which constitute the mass of the garden. [T]here are some tolerable morsels of Grecian architecture & a good ruin."[15] His ideas about both landscape and architecture were being influenced by what he saw in Europe.

Ostensibly to get information for the improvement of rice culture and for the possible introduction of wine-grape and olive growing in America, Jefferson made a trip to northern Italy by way of southern France in 1787. He sent rice, olive trees, and various seeds to South Carolina and Georgia. The rice flourished, but the olive trees failed. No mention was made in his memoranda about gardening or ornamental horticulture on this trip, but his descriptions of the natural beauties were ecstatic. Perhaps it was in Lombardy that he learned to admire the tall poplars that he liked to plant at Monticello. This tree, because of its emphatic shape resembling the Italian cypress, has always appealed to architects (fig. 75).

From reading, Jefferson had come to love Italy before he ever saw it, for when Philip Mazzei came to call on him at Monticello in 1773, Jefferson welcomed him with nostalgic enthusiasm.[16] Mazzei, born amidst the splendor of the Renaissance gardens of Tuscany, was a cultured Italian gentleman who, on account of his horticultural knowledge, had a special appeal for Jefferson. When he stopped off at Monticello in search of a piece of land on which to carry on his experiments with grapes and olives, Jefferson gave him 2,000 acres adjoining his own property in 1774. The friendship that began with the presentation of plants and seeds Mazzei had brought with him

[15] Betts, *Thomas Jefferson's Garden Book*, p. 111; Dos Passos, *The Head and Heart of Thomas Jefferson*, p. 327.

[16] Richard C. Garlick, *Philip Mazzei* (Baltimore and London, 1933), pp. 39–43.

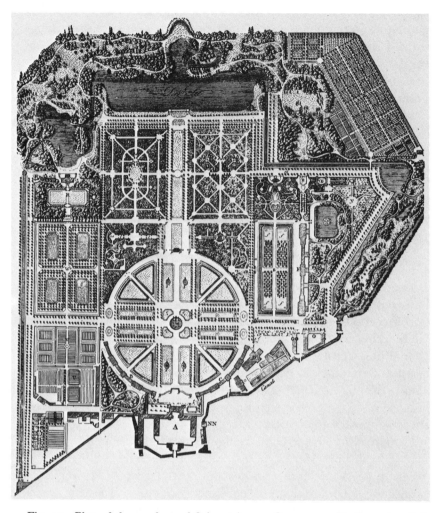

Fig. 74. Plan of the gardens of Schwetzingen, Germany, with the naturalistic alterations of the perimeter gardens and the formal designs commented on by Jefferson (from Marie Louise Gothein, *A History of Garden Art*, London: J. M. Dent & Sons, n.d.)

from Europe lasted a lifetime. The place he built for his experiments was called Colle. He had brought with him "about a dozen laborers of his own country, bound to serve him four or five years." Twenty years later Jefferson recollected: "We made up a subscription for him of 2000 pounds sterling, and he began his experiment. . . .The war

Fig. 75. Monticello, showing Lombardy poplars, a favorite of Jefferson's, as planted by the Thomas Jefferson Memorial Foundation (Frank J. Davis, photographer)

then came on, the time of his people soon expired, some of them enlisted, some chose to settle on other lands . . . some were taken away by the gentlemen of the country for gardeners, so that there did not remain a single one." Jefferson's son-in-law Thomas Mann Randolph described one of these gardeners, "Giovannini," as "an excellent gardener and one of the most sober, industrious men I ever knew."[17]

Mazzei's influence at Monticello was shown by the Italian names Jefferson gave the plants while he was there, and these two gardeners continued a lifelong exchange of plants and seeds. But when Mazzei became an American citizen and was sent abroad to transact business for the state of Virginia, his home, Colle, was rented to the Hessian general Riedesel, "whose horses in one week destroyed the whole labor of three or four years." This disaster plus the ravages of Virginia frosts ended the wine and olive experiments. Nevertheless, Jefferson had had the satisfaction of trying to produce olives in this country. About the olive he wrote, "Of all the gifts of heaven to man, it is next to the most precious, if it be not the most precious"; "after bread, I know no blessing to the poor, in this world, equal to that of oil."[18] The poor were ever close to his heart.

Even though the Mazzei experience was a costly horticultural failure, it did not discourage the maestro of Monticello. His admiration for Italian culture remained unabated. The experiment had been made at his personal expense in the high hope of benefiting American agriculture. If this objective was lost, he at least gained a valued friend whose integrity he never doubted.

Through horticulture Jefferson made friends from all parts of the world, thereby learning things about their cultures which he introduced to the landscape culture of America. He brought ancient Egyptian acacias into his horticultural collection at Monticello. It was an odd coincidence that Jefferson, unaware of the ancient history of *Acacia nilotica*, had fallen in love with a tree imported to Egypt twenty-five centuries earlier by Queen Hatshepsut. None of the many specimens of this beautiful golden flowering acacia that Jefferson bought have survived, but the record of his admiration is clear. His Garden Book entry for May 1778 says: "bought two Aegyptian Acacias (Mimosa Nilotica) from the Gardner at Greenspring. they are from seeds planted March 1777." He referred to it as "the most delicious flowering shrub in the world" and said, "In fact the Mimosa Nilotica & Orange are the only things I ever proposed to have in my

[17] Betts, *Thomas Jefferson's Garden Book*, pp. 63, 203.
[18] Ibid., pp. 63, 120, 145.

green house."[19] He was referring to what is now called his greenhouse, or workshop, connected with the library suite at Monticello (fig. 76). Jefferson was under the illusion that there were two similar species of acacia, "Nilotica & Farnesiana,"[20] until his friend William Hamilton convinced him that *farnesiana* was the correct, and only, name; he used it from then on. As a self-motivated horticultural missionary, he sent many specimens of this plant to friends, including the governor of Georgia, who could probably grow it out of doors as it grows in Greece and Italy.

One of Jefferson's most practical and beautiful contributions to the American landscape was the hawthorn hedge (fig. 77). In 1808 he explained to Hamilton that he had never seen it except around Washington; it "is peculiar at least to America & is a real treasure. as a thorn for hedges nothing has ever been seen comparable to it certainly no thorn in England which I have ever seen makes a hedge any more to be compared to this than a log hut to a wall of freestone." The previous year he had bought from his nurseryman friend, Thomas Main of Georgetown, "4 thousand American Hedge Thorns 6 Doll per M. $24.00" that he had planted at Monticello according to Main's "complete instructions how to plant them." The tree that Main called "American Hedge Thorn" was identified by Linnaeus as *Crataegus cordata* but is now known as *Crataegus phaenopyrum*, or Washington thorn.[21]

Until Jefferson had it brought to Virginia the "Paccan Tree" grew, according to his *Notes on the State of Virginia*, "on the Illinois, Wabash, Ohio, and Missisipi." He not only planted many of them at Monticello but was constantly dispersing them to friends both here and abroad. He asked Francis Hopkinson in 1786 "to procure me two or three hundred Paccan nuts from the Western country. I expect they can be got at Pittsburg" from boats that came up the river. To Thomas Mann Randolph, he wrote in 1790, "I send herewith some

[19] Ibid., pp. 77, 83, 175, 381. "Greenspring, near Williamsburg, was the ancient residence of Governor Sir William Berkeley, of three Philips [*sic*] Ludwells, and of William Lee, at one time Minister of the United States to Holland. It was burned by Federal troops in 1862. Jefferson often visited Greenspring when he was in the Williamsburg area and bought plants from the gardener" (ibid., p. 83).

[20] Ibid., p. 434.

[21] Ibid., pp. 365, 342, 299.

Fig. 76. Monticello, "greenhouse or Workshop" with mimosa (the Italian yellow mimosa) and orange trees referred to by Jefferson as "the only things I ever proposed to have in my green house" (conjectural sketch by Ralph E. Griswold)

seeds which I must trouble you with the care of. they are seeds of the Sugar maple and the Paccan nuts. be so good as to make George prepare a nursery in a proper place and to plant in it the Paccan nuts immediately."[22] Many a Virginia garden and lawn is now shaded by

[22] Jefferson, *Notes on the State of Virginia*, p. 39; Betts, *Thomas Jefferson's Garden Book*, pp. 109, 155.

Fig. 77. *Crataegus phaenopyrum*, formerly *Crataegus cordata*, hawthorn hedge, planted by the thousands at Monticello as directed by Jefferson (photo from Eisler's Nurseries, Butler, Pennsylvania)

pecan trees as a result of this pioneer plant distributor's interest.

The tribute that probably pleased Jefferson as much as any was the naming for him of the native Virginia flower *Jeffersonia diphylla* (fig. 78). On May 18, 1792, Benjamin Smith Barton read a paper before the American Philosophical Society, assembled in Philadelphia, giving the name *Jeffersonia* to a plant which previously had been called *Podophylluv diphyllum*. In his proposal Barton said, "I beg leave to observe to you, in this place, that in imposing upon this genus the name of Mr. Jefferson, I have had no reference to his political character, or to his reputation for general science and for literature. My business was with his knowledge of natural history. In the various departments of this science, but especially in botany and in

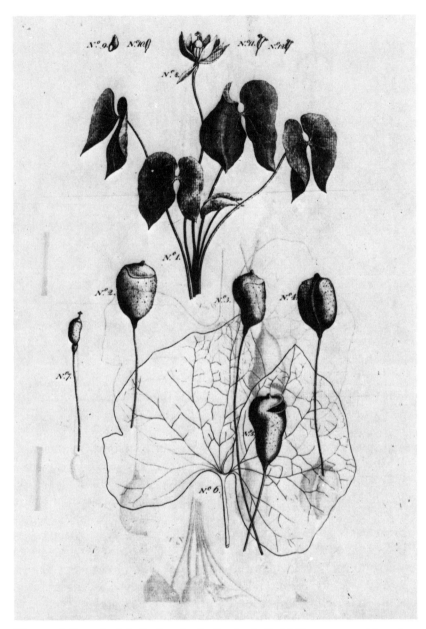

Fig. 78. *Jeffersonia diphylla*, drawing by Benjamin Smith Barton, 1772 (American Philosophical Society)

zoology, the information of this gentleman is equalled by that of few persons in the United-States."[23]

Jeffersonia, a modest flower, was indeed a proper representation of the man for whom it was named. The words of praise from Barton must have been pleasant to the secretary of state who was struggling at that time to get the national capital located on the banks of the Potomac.

[23] Betts, *Thomas Jefferson's Garden Book*, p. 172.

CHAPTER VII

The University of Virginia

Jefferson's design for the University of Virginia was the culmination of his extraordinary life experience—a triumph of intelligent study of architecture, of natural environment, and of human behavior. Having served half a century as statesman and architect for his state and nation, he was well prepared to undertake what was to be his greatest planning accomplishment—the perfect educational institution (fig. 79).

Long before he made any drawings for his future university he wrote in 1810:

the common plan followed in this country of making one large expensive building, I consider as unfortunately erroneous. It is infinitely better to erect a small separate lodge for each separate professorship, with only a hall below for his class, and two chambers above for himself; joining these lodges by barracks for a certain portion of the students, opening into a covered way, to give dry communication between all of the schools. The whole of these arranged around an open square of grass and trees, would make it, what it should be in fact, an academical village.[1]

This spreading out of the academic buildings into the landscape as a unified, harmonious merger of architecture with its natural setting was a new way of thinking that has since become the specialty of landscape architects. To account for this innovation, many architectural historians have tried, without success, to relate this Jeffersonian educational scheme to some previous European institution. As a matter of record the nearest comparable groupings that Jefferson is known to have seen were the Château de Marly near Paris and the Certosa di Pavia in northern Italy (figs. 80, 81). It was while he was infatuated with Maria Cosway that he took her on excursions into the environs of Paris about which he wrote, "how beautiful was every object . . . the hills along the Seine, the rainbows of the machine at Marly, the terrace of St. Germains, the Chateau, the gardens, the

[1] Lipscomb and Bergh, 12: 387.

Fig. 79. Bird's-eye view of Jefferson's "academical village," the University of Virginia (University of Virginia Graphic Communication Services, David M. Skinner, photographer)

statues of Marly." "In Pavia he ate green peas and *admired the Certosa.*"[2] Both of these experiences must have shown him how beautiful and practical a connected group of buildings could be when dedicated to a common purpose such as an "academical village." As Lord Kames noted, at Oxford there was more than one "spacious garden . . . to inspire our youth with a taste not less for simplicity than for elegance."[3]

But the idea of clustering students around a teacher, like iron

[2] Dos Passos, *The Head and Heart of Thomas Jefferson,* pp. 298, 314.
[3] Lord Kames, p. 453.

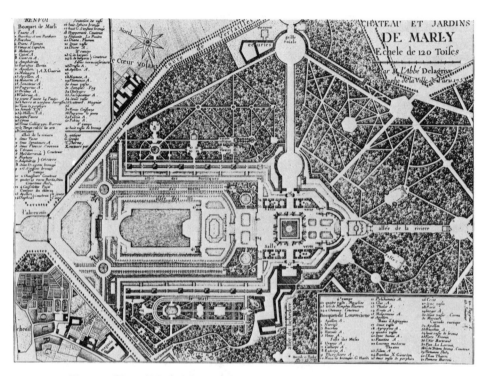

Fig. 80. Plan of Marly (from G. Gromort, *Choix de Plans de Grandes Compositions Exécutées*, Paris: Auguste Vincent, Editeur, 1910)

filings around a magnet, was as old as Plato's Academy, with which, as a classical scholar, Jefferson must have been familiar. Undoubtedly, he knew too about Plato's successor, Aristotle, whose followers, pacing the walks of his Lyceum in the fourth century before Christ, created what has become known as the Peripatetic school. Certainly he was familiar with the great naturalist Theophrastus, who wrote *The Causes of Plants* and established an academic garden of his own in Athens. Teaching in a gardenlike environment was not a modern innovation. But Jefferson glorified it with his imagination. By grouping classrooms with the living quarters of both faculty and students in a unified landscape setting (fig. 82), he created an alternative to the architecture of his alma mater, the College of William and Mary, which had displeased him so.

Concurrent with his thinking about the physical design of his

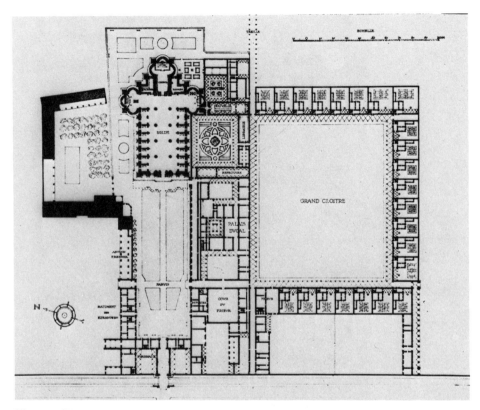

Fig. 81. Plan of the Certosa di Pavia (from Gromort, *Choix de Plans de Grandes Compositions Exécutées*)

"academical village," he outlined his conception of a system of education in a letter to his nephew Peter Carr in 1814. His system included three categories, "1. Elementary Schools, 2. General Schools, 3. Professional Schools." Students were to advance according to ability until only the most able reached the "Professional Schools," in which "each science is to be taught in the highest degree it has attained." In this category he included "the gentleman, the architect, the pleasure gardener, painter and musician to the school of fine arts."[4] If he could

[4] Nathaniel Francis Cabell, *Early History of the University of Virginia as Contained in the Letters of Thomas Jefferson and Joseph C. Cabell*, ed. J. W. Randolph (Richmond, 1856), Appendix B.

Fig. 82. University of Virginia, Böye print, 1828 (Rare Book Department, University of Virginia Library)

have foreseen the specialization that was to take place among the building professions, he would certainly have included landscape architecture in his proposed curriculum.

Another influence in his basic thinking came from his boyhood teacher, the Reverend James Maury, whose aim in teaching was to make each young gentleman a case by himself and "to form his morals & cultivate his genius." For such teaching no more receptive student could have been found than this boy from Shadwell for whom the same objective became his philosophy in planning the University of Virginia. When, at age sixteen, Jefferson was considering going to college, he wrote his guardian, John Harvie, that among practical advantages, "I shall get more universal acquaintance, which may hereafter be serviceable to me; and I suppose I can pursue my studies in the Greek and Latin as well there as here." Referring to this letter, John Dos Passos comments, "Thomas Jefferson was already a man who knew what he wanted to do with his time, with every minute of it . . . his chief pleasure in life was in the affectionate direction of the minds of younger men."[5] Remembering the instructions of the Reverend Mr. Maury and his devoted college professor, Dr. Small, his determination to do likewise for other boys played an important part in his planning for the university.

By the time he was officially authorized to make plans for the university in 1817, he had reached the age of seventy-four and was impatient to get under way. Previously, he had written to Dr. Joseph Priestley in 1800: "We wish to establish in the upper country, and more centrally for the State, an University on a plan so broad and liberal and modern, as to be worth patronizing with the public support, and be a temptation to the youth of other states to come to drink of the cup of knowledge, and fraternize with us." As an early historian of the university explained:

The germ of the University was an incorporated Academy, authorized by law to be established in the county of Albemarle, with the funds to be raised by a lottery, and by private subscription. The contributions from this source, when once begun, having been more speedy and liberal than was expected, (Jefferson himself subscribed $1,000. one of the ten highest contributors) it was enlarged by the same authority into an institution of higher grade, known as the Central College; and before either Academy or

[5] Dos Passos, *The Head and Heart of Thomas Jefferson*, pp. 71, 76, 241.

College had gone into operation, the latter was adopted by the State, liberally endowed and expanded into the seat of science, now known as the University of Virginia.[6]

While Jefferson was serving as president in Washington a man was introduced to him in 1806 who was to be his most valuable assistant in steering the difficult course ahead. That man was Joseph Carrington Cabell, a Virginian who graduated in law from the College of William and Mary in 1798 and because of ill health went to Europe to recover. He remained there three years and, being of scholarly mind, visited universities and studied in all the countries previously visited by Jefferson. He was made to order for the job that the president lost no time in convincing him to undertake. They could discuss with mutual understanding the subject of education and the establishments for its maintenance in those countries. Furthermore, Cabell had attended lectures in botany at Montpellier; these stimulated his interest in the natural sciences generally that was responsible for his "endeavoring to secure a home for [them] in his native State."[7]

As soon as Cabell was back in Williamsburg a proposition for establishing a museum of natural history at the College of William and Mary was presented to him by a foreign scholar, Mr. Del la Coste. Doubting its expedience, Cabell wrote President Jefferson, who replied through his private secretary:

If I could bring myself to consider Williamsburg as the permanent seat of science; as the spot where the youth of our State for centuries to come would go to be instructed in whatever might form them for usefulness, my objection would, in a measure cease. But the old college is declining, and perhaps the sooner it falls entirely, the better, if it might be the means of pointing the way to our legislative body the necessity of founding an institution on an extended and liberal scale . . . and this is what you ought to attempt if you are desirous of doing something which will be of permanent value. . . . instead of wasting your time in attempting to patch up a decaying institution, direct your efforts to a higher and more valuable object. . . . Consent to go into the legislative body.

Fortunately for the University of Virginia, Cabell followed this

[6] Cabell, pp. xix–xxi, xxii.
[7] Ibid., pp. xxiv–xxv.

advice; he "entered the House of Delegates in 1809, where he remained for two years, when he transferred to the Senate."[8] There he became Jefferson's staunch legislative supporter throughout the creation of the University of Virginia. This astute move by Jefferson enabled him to produce what might otherwise never have been achieved, the most comprehensive university plan that had ever been created.

With Cabell's sympathetic influence an act for establishing Central College was passed in February 1816. The Visitors first named by the governor in October of that year were Thomas Jefferson, James Madison, James Monroe, Joseph C. Cabell, John Hartwell Cocke, and David Watson. At a meeting in April 1817 only Jefferson, Cabell, and General Cocke attended, but these three, having examined various sites which had been proposed for the college in the vicinity of Charlottesville, made a conditional choice and purchase of the present location which was approved and ratified by Madison and Monroe at a meeting on May 5, 1817. Jefferson was on his way toward managing to locate his new university away from the Tidewater area which was "exposed to bilious diseases as all the lower country is."[9]

The "Act Establishing University" was not passed until January 25, 1819, after a long debate over potential locations at Lexington, Staunton, and the not-yet-built Central College at Charlottesville. It took the combined tact and political strategy of Cabell and Jefferson to swing the decision in favor of Charlottesville. When it was decided to build a state university in 1818, a bill to that effect was passed by the General Assembly on February 21. The bill appointed the governor and the Council to set up the Rockfish Gap Commission. Beside the site, the commission was also charged with a plan for buildings, a curriculum, the choice of professors, and the measures for governing and organizing the university. These requirements were perfectly in line with Jefferson's thinking and it is quite probable that he had suggested them to Cabell, his devoted friend. Cabell, who was instrumental in setting up the commission, provided for a

[8] Ibid., pp. xxx, xxxi.
[9] J. P. Foley, ed., *The Jeffersonian Cyclopedia*, with introd. by Julian P. Boyd (New York and London, 1967), p. 947.

member from each senatorial district, hoping that this would include both Jefferson and Madison. In one of the most spectacular and beautiful passes of the Blue Ridge at a tavern in the gap (near Afton) the commission met August 1, 1818, and finally selected Charlottesville and its Central College to become the new university.

The first purchase of land at Charlottesville in 1817 was a meager 43¾ acres of what was an old cornfield, described by a ninety-year-old black woman, Kitty Jones, as "that old bald hill where all of us children went to get chinquapins." This baldness must have appealed to the lover of trees from Monticello because the grading required to lay out his plan could be done without destroying any fine old trees. He began hand grading with ten men using spades and hoes, with self-assurance that he knew where every spadeful was going in his ultimate design. He was the surveyor who laid out the work. Gradually more acreage was added, until, by the time the university opened, there was an adequate nucleus of 392⅘ acres.

Immediately following the ratification of the site purchase in 1817, "measures were ... taken for the erection of suitable buildings, according to a plan proposed by Mr. Jefferson, and the corner stone of the first pavilion was laid with appropriate ceremonies on the 6th of October."[10] Up to this point Jefferson had been acting with comprehensive vision in the capacity for which universities engage landscape architects to collaborate with architects. Though there were not enough funds available to carry out the complete plan when Jefferson started, there was not the slightest doubt in his mind about the ultimate composition. From his letters it is clear that for at least thirty-four years before he was able to bring about legislation authorizing the Board of Visitors to proceed, a plan had been developing in his mind. Profiting by the temperamental mistakes of L'Enfant who had lost his opportunity to complete his plans for Washington, Jefferson had planned his legislative strategy no less carefully than his building and grounds.

Appointed by the Visitors to serve with General Cocke as a committee of two "with authority jointly or severally to advise and sanction all plans and application of moneys for executing them," Jefferson had full responsiblity for executing his own plans. The only design instructions he received from the Board were their opinions

[10] Cabell, p. xxv.

"that the ground for these buildings should be previously reduced to a plain or terraces, as it shall be found to admit, with due regard to expense" and "that the pavilions be correct in their architecture and execution."[11]

In their first report to the House of Delegates in 1818, the Visitors stated that "they purchased, at a distance of a mile from Charlottesville, and for the sum of one thousand five hundred and eighteen dollars and seventy-five cents, two hundred acres of land, on which was an eligible site for the college, high, dry, open, furnished with good water and nothing in its vicinity which could threaten the health of the students." These site specifications, obviously Jefferson's, fulfilled all the ecological conditions that are urged by landscape architects in present-day practice. They were the antithesis of the low, damp, unhealthy conditions that Jefferson abhorred at William and Mary. This same report, in addition to repeating Jefferson's description of his "academical village," stated that "this plan offered further advantages of greater security against fire and infection, of extending the buildings in equal pace with the funds, and of adding to them indefinitely hereafter."[12] This agrarian-minded idealist could hardly have been expected to anticipate the expansion of colleges to meet the twentieth-century industrial economy.

Within a few days after he presented his plan to the Board of Visitors he wrote to Dr. William Thornton, architect for the national Capitol, asking for "a few sketches such as need not take you a moment." According to John S. Patton, "a rough drawing accompanied this letter showing the pavilions and dormitories on three sides of the quadrangle" (fig. 83) which was described by Jefferson:

we are commencing here the establishment of a college, and . . . we propose to lay of[f] a square or rather 3. sides of a square about 7. or 800. ft. wide, leaving it open at one end to be extended indefinitely. on the closed end, and on the two sides we propose to arrange separate pavilions for each professor & his school. . . . The whole of the pavilions and dormitories to be united by a colonnade in front, of the height of the lower story of the pavilions & about 8. f. wide under which they may go dry from school to school. . . . Now what we wish is that these pavilions, as they will shew themselves above the Dormitories, should be models of taste and correct architecture and of a

[11] Ibid., p. 397.
[12] Ibid., p. 401.

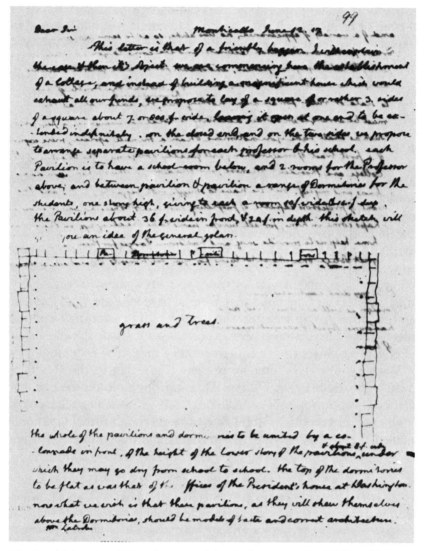

Fig. 83. University of Virginia, general sketch plan sent to Dr. William Thornton by Jefferson, June 12, 1817 (Massachusetts Historical Society)

variety of appearance, no two alike, so as to serve as specimens for the architecutral lectures.[13]

[13] Kimball, *Thomas Jefferson, Architect*, pp. 188, 75.

From this letter it seems plain that there was never the slightest doubt about Jefferson's intended arrangement of the buildings in relation to the landscape. When he wrote to other architects he was merely seeking refinements of his architectural intentions. He had no idea of altering his basic design.

Still searching for excellence of architecture, he also wrote Benjamin Latrobe and was delighted with his suggestion for a focal building, preferably a rotunda, on the third site of the rectangle. Jefferson seized upon this idea by adapting the Pantheon of Rome. He could not reconcile himself to the extravagant use of so much valuable space for a single monumental room and, instead, divided it into a library and a series of splendid oval rooms for classrooms, laboratories, and religious services. It expresses perfectly his philosophy of architectural design: aesthetics as well as function. In working out domestic plans, he loved to adapt them to sloping sites so that one could enter one side at ground level and another side at the level of the first floor. By sinking his Rotunda to the ground level on the north, and raising the steps to the first floor on the south, he managed to retain the resemblance to the Pantheon as the building was seen from the central lawn (fig. 84). But by this device he was also able to provide three oval rooms on the lower floors, as well as a "Dome Room" on the upper floor. The proportions of the latter could then be exactly like those of the Pantheon. Unfortunately, his superb three-story interior burned in 1895. It was replaced by Stanford White with his own unauthentic "improvement" of Jefferson's design. That error was at last rectified by a restoration of the original interior design, completed in 1976. These are the finest such group of oval rooms in American architecture.

As might be expected, the fame of Jefferson's Rotunda as a masterpiece of architectural design has so far overshadowed its distinction as a focal point for his magnificent space conception that its importance to the landscape design has been overlooked.

The addition of the Rotunda to his original scheme had not delayed progress on the rest of the work. It was only five years later that he reported to the Board of Visitors, "the ten pavilions are now almost entirely finished." At the same time he also told them: "The serpentine garden walls between the western range of pavilions and hotels will be finished in two weeks and if weather permits the

Fig. 84. University of Virginia, 1856, lithograph published by C. Bohn showing huge annex added to Jefferson's Rotunda but, fortunately, burned in 1895 and never rebuilt (Manuscript Department, Univesity of Virginia Library)

garden walls on the opposite side will be run up. . . . Considerable progress has been made this summer in digging and leveling the gardens and streets. By the end of the year we shall be nearly through that kind of work."[14] This report leaves no doubt that his entire plan for grounds and buildings was constructed, as he had visualized it, in one inseperable unity. There was in his thinking none of the customary dilemma of "wait until we get the buildings finished before we think about the landscaping."

Speculation about where Jefferson got the idea for the serpentine walls is superfluous. He could have seen them in any number of places in England; in Suffolk alone there are forty-five "crinkle-crankle" walls. It is known that Charles Fenton Mercer built some at his house near Middleburg before 1817.[15] Serpentine walls formed the entrance court of Governor William Berkeley's Greenspring estate near Jamestown, built ca. 1660. Another Tidewater estate, Mannsfield, also had serpentine walls. In England their waving surfaces allowed trees espaliered against them to get enough sun to grow fruit. Jefferson's sketch showing his calculations of the comparative number of bricks required for straight versus serpentine walls shows that his decision was based on economy as well as aesthetics (fig. 85).

Although economy was constantly a factor in his planning, it was not allowed to sway his insistence on appearance. He argued, "Had we built a barn for a college and log huts for accomodations, should we ever have had assurance to propose to an European professor" to come to it?[16] For him, aesthetic as well as academic status constantly guided his decisions at a time when in the United States no other architect or landscape gardener was competent to make comparable design decisions.

The builders were never perplexed for want of interpretation of Jefferson's plans because he was on the job almost daily, riding horseback from Monticello to supervise his own design. When not actually on the site he was overseeing the work by telescope from

[14] John Shelton Patton, *Jefferson, Cabell and the University of Virginia* (New York, 1906), p. 180.

[15] We are indebted to Francis Berkeley, formerly assistant to the President, University of Virginia, for this information.

[16] Patton, p. 260.

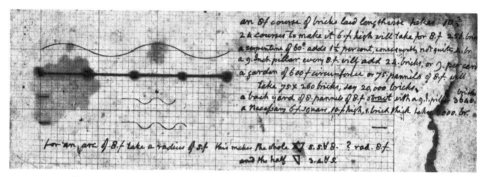

Fig. 85. Drawing by Jefferson of straight and serpentine walls with specifications (Thomas Jefferson Papers, University of Virginia Library)

Monticello. So clear was his three-dimensional vision of his completed design that he could detect and correct the slightest deviation.

To appreciate this phenomenal vision the view of the pavilions from the Rotunda steps gives the most convincing proof. They all seem to be equally spaced, but this is an illusion created by their being spaced farther and farther apart to overcome the normal perspective space recession (figs. 86, 87). Jefferson knew that if he spaced them equally they would appear to become closer and closer together, thus destroying their intended space relation. This was a deliberately contrived optical illusion, called false perspective, which often was used by Renaissance designers. He never mentioned this device, but the actual measurements verify what is shown on the 1822 engraving by Peter Maverick sent to prospective students—a difference of fifty feet in the width of the pavilion gardens at the north and south ends of the lawn. Few if any present-day planners employ this subtlety of space vizualization.

At a meeting of the Board of Visitors in 1822 the following report was agreed to:

all the buildings except one [the Rotunda] have been completed; that is to say, ten distinct houses or pavilions containing each a lecture room, with generally four other apartments for the accomodation of a professor and his family and with a garden and with the requisite family offices [privies]; six hotels for dieting the students, with a single room in each for a refectory . . . a garden and offices for the tenant; and an hundred and nine dormitories,

Fig. 86. University of Virginia, west pavilions as seen from the Rotunda (Frank J. Davis, photographer)

sufficient each for the accomodation of two students, arranged in four distinct rows between the pavilions and hotels, and united with them by covered ways; which buildings are all in readiness for occupation, except . . . the garden walls and grounds to be completed.[17]

A year later it was reported that "these finishings are done." Hence, in 1823 the university construction, with the exception of the Rotunda, was completed as it appears today.

Like the moving of a drama to its climax, the structures most essential to the functioning of the university were completed before

[17] Ibid., p. 472.

Fig. 87. University of Virginia, Pavilion III, showing recently restored Chinese railings (University of Virginia Graphic Communications Services, David M. Skinner, photographer)

the Rotunda which finally closed the gap with dramatic grandeur. Last to be planned and last to be erected, it was, nonetheless, the visual consummation of Jefferson's "academical village." According to Fiske Kimball, "ordered, calm, serene, it stirs our blood with a magic rarely felt on this side of the ocean. It used classic elements, to be sure, but it was not merely imitative. It reaffirmed the supremacy of Form, and worked in the classical spirit of unity, uniformity and balance." [18] High praise, indeed, but still lacking the most significant observation that it united sky, earth, and architecture into a beautiful landscape composition. Of all the appraisals of Jefferson's masterpiece perhaps the most generous was that of George Ticknor of Harvard, who called it "a mass of buildings more beautiful than anything architectural in New England and more appropriate to an University than can be found, perhaps in the world." [19] Characteris-

[18] Kimball, *American Architecture*, p. 84.
[19] Patton, p. 184.

tic of the prevailing supremacy of architecture, no one ever realized that in his particular genius Jefferson was creating a new art not yet defined.

Unfortunately, the vista of the mountains that this potential landscape architect left open at the south end of the lawn was later closed with a building designed by Stanford White, who was not endowed with Jefferson's landscape vision. The closing of Jefferson's vista was, as is so often the situation in "after-planning," an expediency that could not be avoided.

Maverick's engraving of Jefferson's plan shows no trees on the central lawn (fig. 88), but it is ridiculous to suppose that Jefferson intended to leave it bare any more than he meant to leave the gardens unplanted. As a student at William and Mary, he had been surrounded with trees on campus (fig. 89). Any argument that because he left no specific planting plan for the University he did not intend planting trees on the lawn fails to take into account his already demonstrated love of "embellishing grounds by fancy." Documentary proof is, however, not lacking.

In the plan he laid before the Board of Visitors in 1817, "Grass and trees" were noted for the central lawn; the same note was on the sketch he sent to Dr. Thornton only four days after the Board approved his plan (see fig. 83). This was the plan for which the cornerstone of the first building was laid, October 6, 1817, in the presence of three United States presidents, Jefferson, Madison, and Monroe. As Rector of the University, Jefferson paid $1.50 to Mary Gardner in 1823 for 100 young locust trees (fig. 90). That they were planted on the lawn seems probable because forty years later an engraving shows sizable trees that had obviously been growing for some time (figs. 91, 92). Another later source noted that when Professor John A. G. Davis came to the University in 1830, he "found the double rows of young locust trees, which had been planted on each side of the lawn, which were giving promise of shade in years to come."[20] But the most revealing testimony came from Jefferson's architectural understudy, Robert Mills, who in his article on "Architecture in Virginia" published in 1853 by the *Virginia Historical Register* wrote, "The foliage of the trees fronting the buildings on the lawn, and the distance they are apart, separate them to the

[20] *Alumni Bulletin*, 1898, in University of Virginia Library.

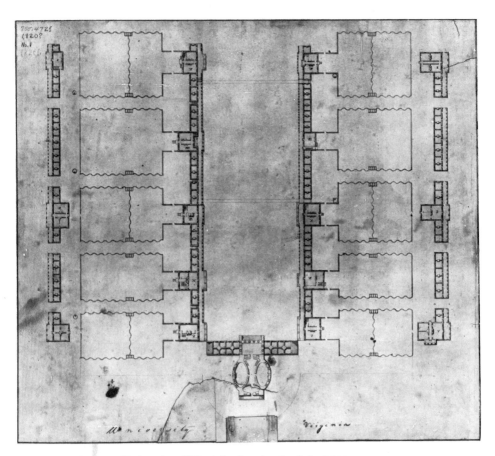

Fig. 88. University of Virginia, drawing by John Neilson and engraving by Peter
Maverick of Jefferson's plan showing the original interior of the Rotunda, 1822
(Virginia State Library)

eye, and associate the idea of a city street, decorated according to
individual taste." This observation of a fellow architect indicates that
the trees he saw were planted so that they did not obscure the
architecture of the pavilions. This would, of course, be a precaution
taken by the architect who designed the buildings.

Much as Jefferson admired the English naturalistic style of gardening, his sense of fitness restrained him from imposing any fake
curvilinear convolutions of contour or quaint clumps of trees and

Fig. 89. College of William and Mary, Williamsburg, Virginia, the restored Wren Building (Colonial Williamsburg Foundation)

bushes in his geometric architectural lawn. His taste was under the control of his judgment. What was appropriate to Monticello was not appropriate to his "academical village."

Two months before his death Jefferson wrote to Dr. John P. Emmet proposing the establishment of a botanical garden on the site where Cabell Hall was later located. In this letter he maintained his capacity for meticulous detail by suggesting the exact site, setting forth its ecological merits, and specifying its size as six acres and the grading of its slope as a series of terraces following the natural contour. He proposed the choice and disposition of the plants and offered to obtain some from M. Thoüin. Shortly thereafter he learned that Thoüin had died two years earlier but his successor was sending seeds to President Madison, who would send them to Charlottes-

Fig. 90. *Robinia pseudoacacia*, black locust, in center (Frank J. Davis, photographer)

ville. The garden, Jefferson wrote, should be enclosed "with a serpentine brick wall"; "this would take about 80,000 bricks and cost $800, and it must depend on our finances whether they will afford that immediately, or allow us, for awhile, but enclosure of posts and rails." The wall, whatever its material, was a necessary defense against roving hogs. He offered lists of native and exotic plants and sources. Oblivious to ill health and impending death, he followed the old maxim, "Those who love to plant and set leave future ages in their debt." He not only planted trees on the lawn but he provided for their

Fig. 91. University of Virginia, Bohn engraving, 1856, showing sizable trees on the central lawn (Edwin M. Betts Collection, University of Virginia Library)

future protection by an insertion in the enactments for the administration of the University: "All willful injury to any plant, shrub, or other plant, within the precincts, shall be punished by fine not exceeding ten dollars, at the discretion of the faculty."[21]

His botanical garden was built and lasted until it was destroyed for the construction of Cabell Hall. It was his final contribution to the planning of the University of Virginia which more than any other educational institution was the work of a single man. He died July 4, 1826, before his great Rotunda was completed, but even after his death his impetus carried on. A park was laid off by the Board in 1827 north of the Rotunda to create a pleasure ground where the faculty and students could obtain their exercise in good weather. For bad weather, they had the covered wings of the Rotunda that Jeffer-

[21] Betts, *Thomas Jefferson's Garden Book*, pp. 619–21: *Regulations*, An Act for the Administration of the University, Oct. 4, 1824, University of Virginia Library.

Fig. 92. University of Virginia, earliest photograph of the central Jeffersonian grounds and Rotunda, 1868 (University of Virginia Library)

son called "gymnasia." The park was to be laid out with suitable walks and trees, and the Proctor was also directed to plant ornamental trees to the north of the Rotunda in an area enclosed by a strong and neat post-and-rail fence. In this location there are now growing large sycamore trees that Professor Betts surmised had been planted at that time (fig. 93). Again, in 1829 all the grounds were to be enlarged and planted with trees and shrubs. The following year it was decided to plant the gardens on the eastern and western portions of the university. The plan was to include a survey and illustrative drawings of the grounds, and it was ordered to plant locusts between the gardens and ranges. Most of these trees were replaced about 1860 with ash and red maples, some of which are still growing; they are, unfortunately, wrongly placed and too dense for their locations. From then on any Jeffersonian influence on the planting was conjectural.

Fig. 93. *Platanus occidentalis*, sycamore, at University of Virginia, supposed to have been planted by Jefferson (Frank J. Davis, photographer)

The gardens as seen today were reconstructed by The Garden Club of Virginia. Peter Maverick's engraving of Jefferson's plan was used to restore the original walls, with the assistance of archaeologist James M. Knight where the walls had been altered in modern times. The interiors of the gardens were planned by Alden Hopkins, landscape architect, in consultation with the Restoration Committee of the Garden Club, Professor Edmund Campbell, and Professor Betts, the man most responsible for preserving Jefferson's record as a gardener and horticulturalist. No plans for the interiors of the gardens were left by Thomas Jefferson; but his other designs, letters, and lists of plants were sufficient evidence for the style of gardens he would have created (fig. 94). Alden Hopkins made the general preliminary plan for both the west and east gardens (fig. 95) and completed the west gardens, which were presented to President Colgate W. Darden, Jr., in 1952 by the president of The Garden Club of Virginia, Mrs. William W. S. Butler. All of the architectural details such as gates, steps, benches, wall restorations, and privies were prepared by the landscape architect as if Jefferson himself had been carrying out his intended design. But, like Jefferson, Hopkins died before his work was completed. Work on the east gardens was postponed until 1960 when Hopkins's assistant on the west gardens, Donald Parker, succeeded him as landscape architect for the east gardens (figs. 96, 97). Here, the wall reconstruction and grading were much more difficult, and the authors of this work were retained as consultants. These gardens, an interpretation of Hopkins's general design, were not completed until 1965, when they were presented to President Edgar F. Shannon, Jr., by Mrs. Wyatt Aiken Williams, president of The Garden Club of Virginia. It is worthy of note that it took two landscape architects and two consultants (an architect and another landscape architect) to restore what Thomas Jefferson could have accomplished single-handedly. Neither before nor since has any one man performed the multiple design functions of surveyor, architect, and landscape architect as skillfully as Thomas Jefferson, who, according to his own epitaph, is memorialized as "Father of the University of Virginia."

Fig. 94. University of Virginia, garden of Pavilion III, typical Jeffersonian *jardin anglais*, with capital from old Rotunda in foreground (Frank J. Davis, photographer)

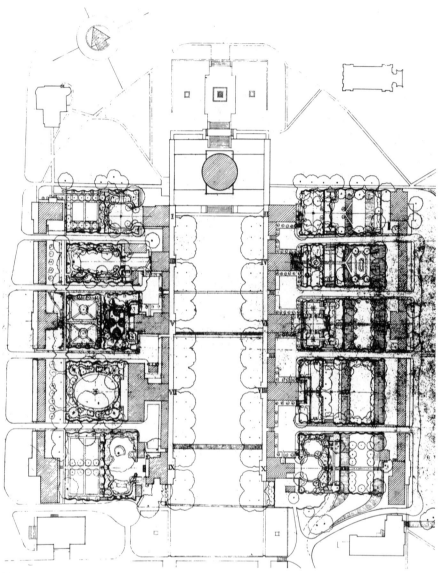

Fig. 95. University of Virginia, proposed garden restoration by The Garden Club of Virginia, designed by Alden Hopkins, landscape architect, 1952 (The Garden Club of Virginia)

Fig. 96. University of Virginia, garden of Pavilion VIII, a full-length view of the central axis (Frank J. Davis, photographer)

Fig. 97. University of Virginia, garden of Pavilion X, 1974, students using garden for study as intended by Jefferson (Frank J. Davis, photographer)

Epilogue

Not since Hadrian of Rome has anyone combined administrative talent with aesthetic genius more successfully than Thomas Jefferson of Monticello.

America needed such a leader. With heart, hand, and mind he created a new kind of government, a new law guaranteeing religious freedom, a new attitude toward education, and a new interpretation of architecture. That interpretation united for the first time all the functions of government and education with the natural landscape and architecture that "had the approbation of thousands of years";[1] Jefferson used what he learned directly from nature, books, and the works of civilized people.

The last third of Jefferson's life was the period of his greatest achievement in landscape architecture. During his years in the presidency, he took advantage of every opportunity to assist the design of the Capitol and of the city of Washington. He even made drawings of his concept of Pennsylvania Avenue and of a layout for the new city on the Potomac.

Monticello was acclaimed by distinguished visitors for its innovations in architecture, gardening, and site planning. For his retreat, Poplar Forest, near Lynchburg, he designed a total environment, the first in American domestic architecture, using a single geometric form, the octagon. The gardens, the terraces, and even the privies took this form.

If Poplar Forest was Jefferson's masterpiece in domestic architecture, the chastely beautiful classical buildings he designed for the University of Virginia were his greatest achievement in public building.

Even though he was seventy-three in 1816, he resumed his "crusade against ignorance" by drawing up legislative bills, investigating courses of study, and designing the buildings for "Central

[1] Padover, pp. 58–59.

College" near Charlottesville. In 1819 it became the University of Virginia, which was to be based "on the illimitable freedom of the human mind to explore and to expose every subject susceptible of its contemplation." [2] Just before he died he was busy planning a professorship in agriculture and a botanical garden, and he was looking for a "good master in the military or landscape line for the University." There were also to be groves of trees of "exotic or distinguished usefulness." [3]

In his life, as in his buildings and gardens, Jefferson's taste was marked by elegant restraint. For him gardens should be beautiful as well as useful, and one was not more important than the other.

Above all Jefferson was a humanitarian. By applying his profound knowledge of nature and his intelligent observation of historic architecture, he was able to plan many houses and assist in the design of a state capitol, a federal city, and a university to fit the needs of our country. He was the pioneer of an art that united the natural landscape with architecture for the glory of a new nation.

With characteristic foresight, Jefferson laid out the family cemetery at Monticello. Leaving nothing to chance, he prepared a sketch for his own tombstone on which he specified "the following inscription, & not one word more" (fig. 98). [4]

'Here was buried
Thomas Jefferson
Author of the Declaration of American Independence
of the Statute of Virginia for religious freedom
& Father of the University of Virginia.'

because by these, as testimonials that I have lived,
I wish most to be remembered [5]

It is said that Jefferson showed a drawing of this tombstone to a friend who asked about all of Jefferson's other great achievements—such as wartime governor of Virginia, secretary of state, minister to France, and president. Jefferson answered those were things the people did for him; he wanted to be remembered for what he did for the people.

[2] Paul L. Ford, ed., *Writings of Thomas Jefferson* (New York, 1892–99), 10: 360.
[3] Lipscomb and Bergh, 16: 165–67.
[4] Frederick D. Nichols and James A. Bear, Jr., *Monticello* (Monticello, Va., 1967).
[5] Lipscomb and Bergh, 1: 262.

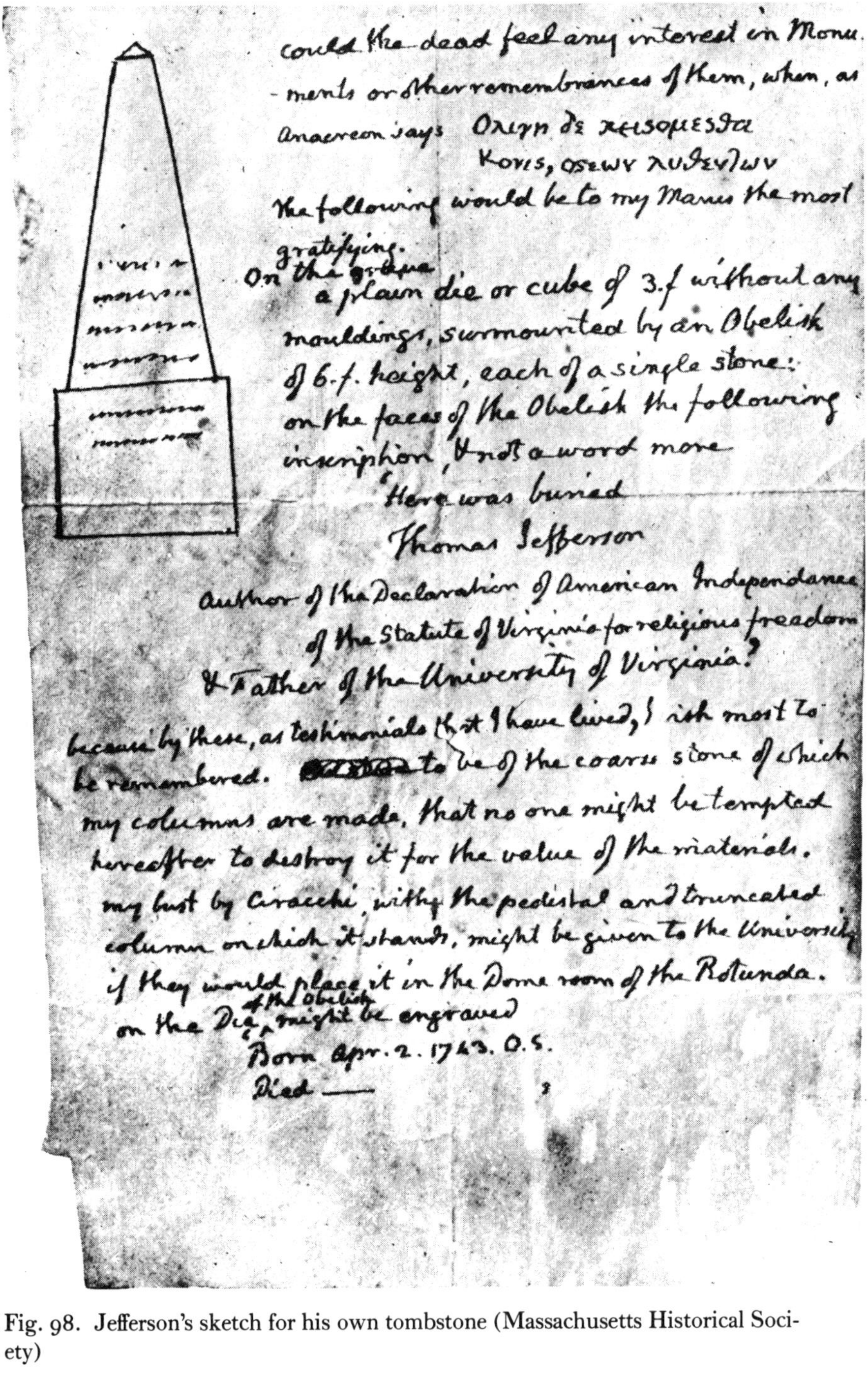

could the dead feel any interest in Monu-
-ments or other remembrances of them, when, as
Anacreon says Ολιγη δε κεισομεσϑα
Κονις, οσεων λυϑεντων
the following would be to my Manes the most
gratifying.
On the grave a plain die or cube of 3.f without any
mouldings, surmounted by an Obelisk
of 6.f. height, each of a single stone:
on the faces of the Obelisk the following
inscription, & not a word more

Here was buried
Thomas Jefferson
Author of the Declaration of American Independance
of the Statute of Virginia for religious freedom
& Father of the University of Virginia.

because by these, as testimonials that I have lived, I wish most to
be remembered. to be of the coarse stone of which
my columns are made, that no one might be tempted
hereafter to destroy it for the value of the materials.
my bust by Ciracchi, with the pedestal and truncated
column on which it stands, might be given to the University
if they would place it in the Dome room of the Rotunda.
on the Die of the Obelisk might be engraved
Born apr. 2. 1743. O.S.
Died ——

Fig. 98. Jefferson's sketch for his own tombstone (Massachusetts Historical Society)

Bibliography

Index

Bibliography

Articles

Dos Passos, John. "Builders for a Golden Age," *American Heritage* 10, no. 5(1959): 65–77.

Kimball, Fiske. "The Building of Bremo," *Virginia Magazine of History* 57 (Jan. 1949): 3–13.

____. "Thomas Jefferson and the First Monument of the Classical Revival in America," *Journal of the American Institute of Architects* 3 (Nov. 1915): 473.

Little, Bryan. "Cambridge and the Campus: An English Antecedent for the Lawn of the University of Virginia," *Virginia Magazine of History and Biography* 79 (April 1971): 3.

McPeck, Eleanor. "George Isham Parkyns," *Quarterly Journal of the Library of Congress* 30 (July 1973): 171–82.

Mills, Robert. "Architecture in Virginia," *Virginia Historical Register*. Richmond, 1853.

True, Rodney H. "Thomas Jefferson in Relation to Botany," *Scientific Monthly*. Rept., Science Press, 1916.

Books

Ackerman, James. *Palladio*. Baltimore: Penguin Books, 1966.

____. *Palladio's Villas*. Locust Valley, N.Y.: J. J. Austin for the Institute of Fine Arts, New York University, 1967.

Alumni Bulletin. Charlottesville: University of Virginia, 1898.

Barlow, Elizabeth, and William Alex. *Frederick Law Olmsted's New York*. New York: Praeger Publishers, 1972.

Bear, James A. *Family Letters of Thomas Jefferson*. Columbia: University of Missouri Press, 1966.

Berman, Eleanor. *Thomas Jefferson among the Arts* (New York, 1947).

Betts, Edwin Morris, ed. *Ground Plan and Prints of the University of*

Virginia. Rept. from *Proceedings of the American Philosophical Society* 90 (1946).

_____. *Thomas Jefferson's Farm Book.* Princeton, N.J.: Princeton University Press, for the American Philosophical Society, 1953. Rept. Charlottesville: University Press of Virginia, 1977.

_____. *Thomas Jefferson's Garden Book, 1766–1824, with Relevant Extracts from His Other Writings.* Philadelphia: American Philosophical Society, 1944.

Betts, Edwin Morris, and Hazelhurst Bolton Perkins. *Thomas Jefferson's Flower Garden at Monticello.* 2d ed. Charlottesville: Univesity Press of Virginia, 1971.

Birch, William. *Autobiography.* Boston: Massachusetts Historical Society; Charlottesville: Thomas Jefferson Memorial Foundation and University of Virginia Press, 1961.

Boyd, Julian P., ed. *The Papers of Thomas Jefferson.* Princeton, N.J.: Princeton University Press, 1950—.

Boykin, Edward. *Thomas Jefferson: To the Girls and Boys. Little-Known Letters of Thomas Jefferson to and from His Children and Grandchildren.* New York: Funk & Wagnalls, 1964.

Bruce, Philip Alexander. *History of the University of Virginia, 1819–1919.* New York: Macmillan Company, 1920–22.

Bullock, Helen Duprey. *My Head and My Heart.* New York, 1945.

Burke, Edmund. *Essay on the Sublime and the Beautiful.* 1757. Rept. Oxford, 1925.

Cabell, Nathaniel Francis. *Early History of the University of Virginia as Contained in the Letters of Thomas Jefferson and Joseph C. Cabell.* Ed. J. W. Randolph. Richmond: J. W. Randolph, Publisher, 1856.

Castell, Robert. *The Villas of the Ancients Illustrated.* London: for the author, 1728.

Chambers, [Sir] William. . . . *Views of the Gardens and Buildings at Kew.* London: J. Haberkorn for the Author, 1763.

Chastellux, marquis de. *Travels in North America, in the Years 1780, 1781, and 1782.* Ed. Howard C. Rice, Jr. Chapel Hill: University of North Carolina Press for the Institute of Early American History and Culture, 1963.

Dezallier d'Argentville, Antoine Joseph [attributed to Alexander Le Blond]. *The Theory and Practice of Gardening.* 2d ed. Trans. John

James. London: Bernard Lintot, 1728. Known as *James on Gardening*.

Dos Passos, John. *The Head and Heart of Thomas Jefferson*. Garden City, N.Y.: Doubleday, 1954.

———. *Thomas Jefferson, The Making of a President*. Boston: Houghton Mifflin, 1964.

Downing, Andrew Jackson. *The Architecture of Country Houses*. New introd. by George B. Tatum. New York: DeCapo Press, 1968.

———. *Theory and Practice of Landscape Gardening*. With the 1859 6th ed. supplemented by Henry Winthrop Sargent. New York: Funk & Wagnalls, 1967.

Dumbauld, Edward. *Thomas Jefferson, American Tourist*. Tulsa: University of Oklahoma Press, 1946.

Ewan, Joseph, and Nesta Ewan. *John Banister and His Natural History of Virginia, 1678–1692*. Urbana: University of Illinois Press, 1970.

Foley, J. P., ed. *The Jeffersonian Cyclopedia*. With introd. by Julian P. Boyd. New York and London: Funk & Wagnalls, 1967.

Ford, Paul L., ed. *Writings of Thomas Jefferson*. New York: G. P. Putnam's Sons, 1892–99.

Frary, I. T. *Thomas Jefferson, Architect and Builder*. Richmond: Garrett & Massie, 1931.

Garlick, Richard C. *Philip Mazzei*. Baltimore: The Johns Hopkins Press; London: Oxford University Press, 1933.

Garrett, Wendell D., and Joseph C. Farber (photographer). *Jefferson Redivivus*. Barre, Mass.: Barre Publishers, 1971.

Gibbs, James. *A Book of Architecture*. London, 1728.

Hamilton, J. G. DeRoulhac. *The Best Letters of Thomas Jefferson*. Boston: Houghton Mifflin Company, 1926.

Hamlin, Talbot. *Greek Revival Architecture in America*. 1944. Rept., New York: Dover Publications, 1964.

Heely, Joseph. *Letters on the Beauties of Hagley. . . .* London: R. Baldwin, 1777.

Hogarth, William. *The Analysis of Beauty*. 1753. Rept., ed. Joseph Burke, Oxford: The Clarendon Press, 1955.

Indiana Works Progress Guide. New York: Oxford University Press, 1941.

Jefferson, Issac. *Memoirs of a Monticello Slave.* Ed. James A. Bear. Charlottesville, Va.: Thomas Jefferson Memorial Foundation, 1955.

Jefferson, Thomas. *Autobiography of Thomas Jefferson.* With introd. by Dumas Malone. New York: Capricorn Books, n.d.

_____. *Notes on the State of Virginia.* Ed. William Peden. Chapel Hill: University of North Carolina Press for the Institute of Early American History and Culture, 1955.

_____. *The Jefferson Bible.* Ed. O. I. A. Roche and C. N. Potter. St. Louis and Chicago: Thompson Publishing Co., 1902.

Kames, Henry Home, Lord. *Elements of Criticism.* Vol. 2. 1762. Rept. Edinburgh, 1774.

Kimball, Marie. *Jefferson: The Road to Glory.* New York: Coward-McCann, 1943.

Kimball, Fiske. *American Architecture.* Indianapolis: Bobbs-Merrill Company, 1928.

_____. *The Creation of the Rococo.* Philadelphia, 1943.

_____. *Thomas Jefferson, Architect.* 1916. Rept., with introd. by Frederick D. Nichols, New York: DaCapo, 1968.

Lambeth, William Alexander, and Warren H. Manning. *Thomas Jefferson as an Architect and a Designer of Landscapes Primarily Based on University of Virginia and Monticello.* Boston and New York: Houghton Mifflin Company, 1913.

LeRouge, Goerge Louis. *Des Jardins Anglo-Chinois.* Paris: Le Rouge Publishers, 1776–88.

Lipscomb, Andrew A., and Albert E. Bergh. *Writings of Thomas Jefferson.* Monticello edition. Washington, D.C.: Thomas Jefferson Memorial Association, 1903.

Loudon, John Claudius. *A Treatise on Farming, Improving and Managing Country Residences.* 1806. Rept. Westmeade, Eng.: Gregs International, 1971.

McMahon, Bernard. *The American Gardener's Calendar.* 11th ed. Philadelphia: J. B. Lippincott & Company, 1857.

Malone, Dumas. *Jefferson and the Ordeal of Liberty.* Boston: Little Brown and Company, 1962.

_____. *Jefferson the President: Second Term, 1805–1809.* Boston: Little Brown and Company, 1974.

_____. *Jefferson and the Rights of Man.* Boston: Little Brown and Company, 1951.

———. *Jefferson the Virginian*. Boston: Little Brown and Company, 1948.

Mayo, Bernard. *Jefferson Himself*. Boston: Houghton Mifflin Company, 1942.

Miller[–ar], Philip. *Dictionaire des Jardiniers*. Paris, 1785.

———. *Gardener's Calendar*. London: Philip Miller, 1765.

———. *The Gardener's and Florist's Dictionary*. London, 1731; rept. 1765, 1768.

Mississippi Writers Guide. New York: Viking, 1938.

Newton, Norman T. *Design on the Land*. Cambridge, Mass., 1971.

Nichols, Frederick Doveton. *Thomas Jefferson's Architectural Drawings*. 1961. Rev. and enl. 3d ed., Boston: Massachusetts Historical Society; Charlottesville: University Press of Virginia, 1971.

———, and James A. Bear, Jr. *Monticello*. Monticello, Va.: Thomas Jefferson Memorial Foundation, 1967.

Olmsted, Frederick Law, Sr. *Forty Years of Landscape Architecture*. Ed. Frederick Law Olmsted, Jr., and Theodora Kimball. New York and London: G. P. Putnam's Sons, 1928.

Padover, Saul K. *The Complete Jefferson*. New York, 1943.

———. *Thomas Jefferson and the National Capital . . . , 1783–1818*. Washington, D.C.: G.P.O. 1946.

Palladio, Andrea. *I quatro libri dell' architettura*. Venice: Appresso Bartolomeo, Carampello, 1581.

———. The Architecture of A. Palladio in Four Books. Revised, designed, and published by Giacomo Leoni. London: John Watts, 1715.

Parkyns, G. F. *Six Designs for Improving and Embellishing Grounds with Sections and Explanations*. London: I. and J. Taylor, 1793. *Bound with* John Soane. *Sketches in Architecture Containing Plan and Elevations of Cottages, Villas, and Other Useful Buildings with Characteristic Scenery*. Copy at Dumbarton Oaks Garden Library, Washington, D.C.

Patton, John Shelton. *Jefferson, Cabell and the University of Virginia*. New York, 1906.

———. *Jefferson's University*. Charlottesville, Va., 1915.

Pliny the Second. *Letters and Panegyricus*. Tr. Betty Radice. Cambridge, Mass., 1969.

Randall, Henry S. *Life of Thomas Jefferson*. 139th ed. Richmond: Randall Publishers, 1858.

Randolph, Sara N. *The Domestic Life of Jefferson*. Charlottesville, Va., 1934.

Reps, John W. *Tidewater Towns: City Planning in Colonial Virginia and Maryland*. Williamsburg, Va.: Colonial Williamsburg Foundation, 1972.

Seeley, B. *Stowe: A Description*. New ed. Buckingham, Eng.: B. Seeley, 1783.

Shenstone, William. *Shenstone's Works*. Vol. 2. 1764. Rept., London, 1773.

Sowerby, E. Millicent, ed. *Catalogue of the Library of Thomas Jefferson*. Washington, D.C., 1952–59.

Thurlow, Constance E., et al., comps. *The Jefferson Papers of the University of Virginia*. 2 parts. Charlottesville: University Press of Virginia, 1973.

Van Loon, Hendrick Willem. *Thomas Jefferson*. New York: Dodd, Mead & Company, 1943.

Vaux, Calvert. *Villas and Cottages: A Series of Designs Prepared for Execution in the United States*. New York: Harper & Brothers, 1857.

Whately, Thomas. *Observations on Modern Gardening*. London: T. Payne, 1770.

Whiffen, Marcus. *The Public Buildings of Williamsburg*. Williamsburg, Va.: Colonial Williamsburg Foundation, 1958.

Index

Page numbers in *italics* refer to illustrations.